AF888974

Business Basics

David Grant and Robert McLarty

Oxford University Press 1995

Contents

Grammar	Vocabulary	Functions	Revision
The Present Simple tense *He does. He doesn't. Does he...?*	Nationalities	Checking spelling	
Information questions *What...? Where...? How many...?*	Company activities *manufacture* *make* *employ*		
Yes/no questions *Is it...? / Does it...?*	**Numbers** *figures, prices, years*	Checking numbers	Information questions
Adverbs of frequency *always sometimes never*	Leisure activities *go play do*		
Question forms *Is there...? Are there...? How many...?*	Hotel facilities	Asking for information	
	Hotel reservation	**Making requests** *Can I...? Could you...?*	
Time questions *When? What time? How long?*	Flight reservation	**Telling the time** *a quarter past six* *6.15 p.m. 18.15*	Numbers
Countable and uncountable nouns *How much...?* *How many...?*		Checking in to a hotel	Making requests
	Telephone language 1	**Suggesting, accepting, and refusing** *Shall we...?* *Would you like to...?*	
Prepositions	Maps	**Giving directions** *It's opposite... Go past... Turn left...*	Information questions
	Restaurant language *I'd like...* *I recommend...*	Ordering, complaining, paying	Countable and uncountable nouns
The Past Simple tense *He went. He didn't go. Did he go?*			Question forms
	Vocabulary for socializing 1	**Introductions and conversation openers** *Welcome to...* *Pleased to meet you.*	
	Company departments *Sales, Personnel, Production*	**Describing company organization** *division subsidiary parent company*	

1

You and your company

1.1 People in business

The Present Simple tense

He does. *He doesn't.* *Does he... ?*

SEE LANGUAGE FILES: 2, 10, 11

A **LISTENING**

This is Olaf Olafsson. He works for Sony in the United States. He is President of Sony's video game division, but he is only 30 years old. He also has a very interesting hobby.

1 a What is unusual about Olaf Olafsson?

b What do you think Olaf Olafsson's 'very interesting hobby' is?

2 Miguel Martinez, a Spanish journalist, is interviewing Mr Olafsson. Listen to the interview and complete the information on Miguel's notepad.

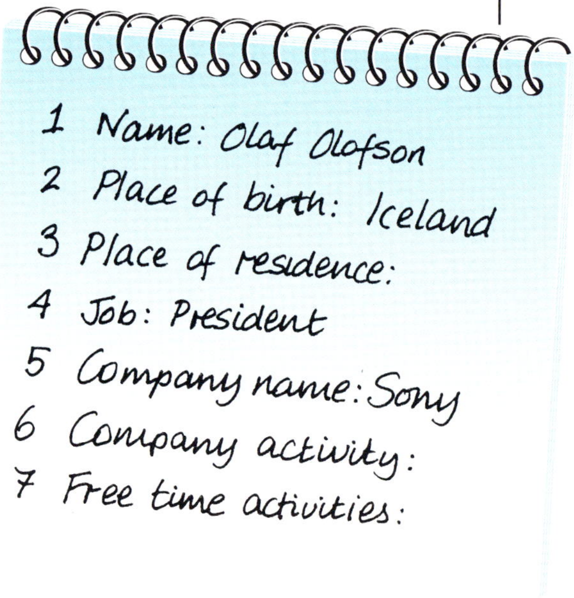

3 What questions does Miguel Martinez ask? With a partner, write down the questions you remember.

4 Listen again to check your answers.

B

PRACTICE

1 Match questions a-g with numbers 1-7 on Miguel Martinez's notepad in A **1**. The first one is done for you.

a Where are you from? ..2..
b Who do you work for? ....
c What do you do in your free time? ....
d Where do you live? ....
e What do you do? ....
f What's your surname/first name? ....
g What does your company do? ....

2 Now ask and answer questions a-g with a partner.

○ *Where are you from?*
● *I'm from Japan. And you?*
○ *I come from France.*

LANGUAGE NOTE

The Present Simple

When we talk about regular or permanent actions, we use the Present Simple tense.
I write books. I work for Sony.

1 In the question and negative forms, we use *do* and *don't*.
Do *you work at weekends?*
Where ***do*** *you work?*
I ***don't*** *take my work home.*

2 In the third person (*he, she, it*) form, the verb takes an *s*. In the question and negative forms, we use *does* and *doesn't*.
He works for Sony.
Does *he work at home?*
Where ***does*** *he work?*
He ***doesn't*** *live in Iceland.*

3 With the verb *to be* we do not use *do/don't*.
Where ***are*** *you from?*
You ***aren't*** *from America.*

C READING

This is an extract from the article Miguel Martinez writes about Olaf Olafsson. Fill in the spaces with one of these verbs.

are   is   does   do   don't   isn't   write   writes   works   makes

MEET SONY'S BEST-SELLING PRESIDENT

Sony Electronic Publishing is a division of Sony. It .... (1) video games and software. The President of the division .... (2) old – in fact he is only 30 years old! And his name .... (3) Olaf Olafsson.

But .... (4) you know his other job? In his free time, Olaf Olafsson .... (5) novels and short stories? In his native country, Iceland, Olafsson's books are bestsellers. But if you .... (6) live in Iceland, don't worry! His new novel, *Absolution,* is translated into English and German. And the books .... (7) in the shops now!

Olafsson is a busy man. He .... (8) long hours, and he travels all over the world for Sony. So how .... (9) he find time to write?

'I usually write for an hour or two every evening,' he says. 'And at weekends, I often .... (10) for eighteen hours, alone, on the roof of my apartment building.'

D PRONUNCIATION

It's Olafsson. O-L-A-F-S-S-O-N

1 Work with a partner. Spell your name and first name, and the name and address of your company or school.

2 Now complete this table.

/eɪ/	/i:/	/e/	/aɪ/	/əʊ/	/u:/	/ɑ:/
A	B	F	I	O	Q	R
H	C	L				

3 Now say the following:

BASF JFK BP
ICL GB USA RTZ
BBC JVC

Think of some other common abbreviations in your language. How do you say them in English?

E

LISTENING

Miguel Martinez has two more interviews with business people. Listen and complete the details.

	name	first name	nationality	company
1	....	....	....	....
2	....	Alan	....	....

F

VOCABULARY AND PRONUNCIATION

1 Where are you from? And what nationality are you?

2 Can you name:
a The countries in the European Community?
b The countries in ASEAN?
c The G7 countries?

3 Make a list of:
a Items you have in your office or home.
b Things you are wearing.

Now say where they come from.
I have a Japanese CD player / an English shirt.

4 Complete this table.

Country	Nationality	Country	Nationality
Spain	Spanish		Portuguese
Italy			Belgian
Brazil		Japan	
Canada			Russian
	German	France	
	Hungarian	Korea	
	Mexican	The USA	
	Dutch	Great Britain	
Sweden			Norwegian
Poland			Thai
Turkey			

5 Now listen to some of the words. Where is the main stress or accent on each word? Write it in the correct column. The first one is done as an example.

■ - -	
■ -	Spanish
- ■	
- - ■	
- ■ - -	
- ■ -	

1.2 Talking about your company

Information questions

What... ?   Where... ?   How many... ?

SEE LANGUAGE FILE: 10

A LISTENING AND SPEAKING

A Director of Starbucks, an American coffee manufacturer, is giving a talk about his company.

1 Listen, and choose the correct answer, a or b.

Activity:	a	Sells coffee in the USA and Canada.	b	Sells coffee all over the world.
Location of stores:	a	West Coast	b	West and East Coast
Head Office:	a	Seattle	b	Washington DC
Annual sales:	a	$225 million	b	$285 million
Annual growth:	a	More than 5%	b	More than 75%
Name of President:	a	Mr Howard	b	Mr Schultz
Employees:	a	3,500	b	6,000
Company philosophy:	a	Customer comes first.	b	Customer and employee both come first.

2 Think about some companies you know well. Does the customer come first, or the employee? In your opinion, which is better?

3 Is it a good idea for employees to have shares in their company?

B

VOCABULARY

Here are some facts about Starbucks. Use the words in the box to complete the second sentence, so that it means the same as the first. The first one is done for you.

located based sells sales employs ~~manufactures~~ specialize

1 The company produces a brand of coffee.
It ...*manufactures*... a brand of coffee.
2 In particular, we produce high-quality coffee.
We .... in high-quality coffee.
3 Starbucks' customers buy their coffee in 400 stores.
Starbucks .... coffee in 400 stores.
4 Our turnover for this year is $285million.
We have .... of $285million this year.
5 The head office of the company is in Seattle.
The company is .... in Seattle.
6 We have many stores on the West Coast.
Many of our stores are .... on the West Coast.
7 6,000 people work for the company.
The company .... 6,000 people.

LANGUAGE NOTE

Presenting your company

Where it is
The company is based in...
The head office is in...
Our subsidiary/factory/office is located in...

Products and services
My company specializes in...
Our main products are...
We manufacture/produce/make...
We sell...

Size
We have annual sales of...
Our annual turnover is...
We employ...

C

SPEAKING

Now use expressions in the Language Note to present your own company, or a company you know well.

D

QUESTION-MAKING

Here are some questions about companies. Put the words in the right order.

1 name the company your is What of ?
2 does company What the do ?
3 the located Where company is ?
4 sales What company's the annual are ?
5 does company many How employ the people ?

E

PAIR WORK

Person A: Your information is in File A, page 156.

Person B:

1 Your partner works for a big company. Ask your partner questions to get more information. Complete this table.

Company	
Activity	
Location	
Turnover	
Sales	

2 You work for the company below. Answer your partner's questions.

The company is ITT. It employs a total of 110,000 people. It has its headquarters in the USA, but 30% of its employees work in Europe. It specializes in products for the defence, electronics, and motor industries. It has annual sales of more than $20 billion.

F

PRACTICE

Now write a paragraph like the one in E **2** about your company, or about a well-known company.

1.3 Company facts and figures

Numbers
figures, prices, years

SEE LANGUAGE FILES: 1, 11

A READING

1 What do you know about Swatch watches? (Where are they from? How much do they cost?)

2 Are these sentences true (T) or false (F)?

		T	F
a	The head office of the company is in Munich, Germany.	☐	☐
b	Swatch and Omega are sister companies.	☐	☐
c	There are ten new designs of Swatch watches every year.	☐	☐
d	The company sells 35,000 Swatch watches a year.	☐	☐
e	The Swatch factory never closes.	☐	☐
f	The price of a Swatch watch is the same as in 1983.	☐	☐
g	The President of the company wants to produce a Swatch car.	☐	☐

3 Now read the text and check your answers.

TIME IS MONEY

This is Nicolas Hayek, the founder and President of SMH. SMH is a Swiss watch manufacturer with its head office in Zurich, Switzerland, and a large, modern factory in Granges, France. It employs 14,000 people. There are twelve companies in the group, including Tissot, Omega, and Swatch.

The company's most famous product is the Swatch watch. The Swatch has a quartz mechanism but only fifty-one parts. A new collection comes out twice a year with forty new designs. SMH sells ten million Swatch watches a year.

The factory in Granges is open twenty-four hours a day, with a daily production of 35,000 watches. Created in 1983, the company makes large profits every year, but a Swatch watch still only costs £25, the same price as in 1983.

Nicolas Hayek is now sixty-five, but he has no plans to retire. One day he hopes to produce the Swatch car, a revolutionary automobile for the next century. But it's not 'all work and no play' for Mr Hayek. In his free time he plays a lot of tennis, sometimes with his friend Jean-Paul Belmondo, the French actor.

B

QUESTION-MAKING

Complete the questions and answers as in the examples. Look at the text in A to help you.

○ *Is SMH a Swiss company?*
● *Yes, it is.*
○ *Does Swatch make cars?*
● *No, it doesn't. It makes watches.*

1 ○ .... the head office of SMH in Basle?
● .... , it .... It .... in Zurich.
2 ○ .... there fourteen companies in the group?
● .... , there .... There .... twelve.
3 ○ .... Swatch watches .... fifty-one parts?
● .... , they ....
4 ○ .... a new collection come out once a year?
● .... , it .... It .... out twice a year.
5 ○ .... the factory open 24 hours a day?
● .... , it ....
6 ○ .... the factory produce 35,000 watches a year?
● .... , it .... It .... 35,000 a day.
7 ○ .... Nicolas Hayek .... plans to retire?
● .... , he ....
8 ○ .... Nicolas Hayek and Jean-Paul Belmondo .... golf?
● .... , they .... They .... tennis.

C

LISTENING

1 Cover up the TIME IS MONEY text on page 16. Listen and write down the numbers you hear.

2 Now uncover the text and check your answers.

D

PRACTICE

Write the numbers below using figures. The first one is done for you.

a nineteen pounds sixty-five *£19.65*
b one million nine hundred (and) sixty-five thousand
c nine
d nineteen sixty-five
e one thousand nine hundred (and) sixty-five
f ninety
g six hundred (and) ninety-five
h nineteen

LANGUAGE NOTE

Saying numbers

1 These numbers are often confused.

13	*thirteen*	30	*thirty*
14	*fourteen*	40	*forty*
15	*fifteen*	50	*fifty*
16	*sixteen*	60	*sixty*
17	*seventeen*	70	*seventy*
18	*eighteen*	80	*eighty*
19	*nineteen*	90	*ninety*

See Language File 1, page 163 for a more complete list of numbers.

2 The words *hundred* and *thousand* are always used without an *s*.

200 *two hundred*
3,000 *three thousand*

In British English, the word *hundred* is followed by *and*. In American English, it isn't.

432 *four hundred and thirty-two* (British)
four hundred thirty-two (American)

3 Saying prices:

one pound (£1) = *one hundred pence*

£31	*thirty-one pounds*
90p	*ninety pence / ninety p*
£25.60	*twenty-five pounds sixty*

one dollar ($1) = *one hundred cents*

$79	*seventy-nine dollars*
80¢	*eighty cents*
$41.50	*forty-one dollars fifty*

4 Saying years:

1995 *nineteen ninety-five*
1856 *eighteen fifty-six*
2006 *two thousand and six*

E

LANGUAGE FOCUS

1 Say the numbers, prices, and dates below

Numbers: 7 5 17 15 70 50 172 359
1,965 3,400 8,212 13,000,000 8,732,000

Prices: £17.50 £19.65 $230.60

Dates: 1789 1993 1965 1066

2 Now listen and check your answers.

F

PRACTICE

1 Listen to the five sentences (a-e) and say which number you hear.

a five or nine?
b thirteen or thirty?
c sixteen or sixty?
d eighteen or eighty?
e nineteen or ninety?

2 Fill in the gaps in sentences 1-6 with the numbers below.

8.05
805
19.65
1965
1,965
1,965,000

1 I was born in ....
2 The current exchange rate is just over eight French francs to the pound – .... FF to be exact.
3 I'm afraid I've only got twenty pounds in cash. That's OK, the bill is for £.............. .
4 The company has .... employees, and we hope to have a thousand employees soon.
5 We have .... stores worldwide, and our two-thousandth store opens next year.
6 He has .... shares in the company – just under two million.

Now say the sentences.

G

SPEAKING

Think about the country/town where you are studying now. Answer these questions with a partner.

1 What's the population of the country? And of the town?
2 How many towns are there in the country with more than a million people?
3 What's the year of the last Presidential or government election in the country? What year is the next election?
4 What's the price of a two-bedroom flat/apartment in the centre of town?
5 How much do you pay to travel on public transport in town? And how much do you pay to park your car in the centre of town?

1.4 Work and leisure

Adverbs of frequency

always *sometimes* *never*

A

WRITING AND LISTENING

1 Read the information below. For each person, answer these questions.

a What nationality are they?
b Where do they live?
c What do they do?

ALAN YENTOB

Alan Yentob is the Controller of BBC1, the British television station. He lives in Notting Hill in London with the film-maker Philippa Walker and their two-year old son Jacob.

AGNÈS B

Agnès B is a fashion designer, and the founder of 'Agnès B', which has clothes shops in Paris and London. She lives and works in her home town of Paris.

2 Now write about your partner in the same way. Before you start writing, ask your partner questions to get the information you need.

3 Write two sentences about a famous person, but don't say who it is. Read your sentences to your partner or to the class. Can they guess who it is?

Miguel Martinez is interviewing Alan Yentob and Agnès B.

4 Before you listen, look at the sentences (1-11) below. Which person do you think says each sentence? Alan Yentob or Agnès B?

1 I often have lunch in the office – usually a sandwich.
2 I watch last night's TV programmes on video.
3 We cook dinner at home for friends.
4 I sometimes have breakfast meetings in a small hotel near my office.
5 I usually arrive at our office on rue Dieu at 10.30.
6 When we prepare the new collections, we have dinner at work.
7 I go swimming with my son.
8 At home, I sometimes try on new clothes in front of the mirror.
9 I sometimes play tennis.
10 I never go into a clothes shop.
11 I never go to bed before one or two in the morning.

5 Now listen and write the sentences above in the order you hear them. The first one is done for you.

Alan Yentob	*2*
Agnès B	

B

LANGUAGE FOCUS

Alan Yentob and Agnès B use words like *sometimes*, *usually*, and *never* to describe how often they do things.

Look at the Tapescript on page 177-8. What other similar words can you find?

LANGUAGE NOTE

Adverbs of frequency

100%		*always*	
		usually	
		normally	
	I	*often*	*eat in a restaurant.*
		sometimes	
		occasionally	
		rarely	
0%		*never*	

C PRACTICE

Talk about your daily routine with a partner. Use sentences 1-11 in A for ideas.
I always have lunch in my office.

Use these adverbs:
always usually often sometimes occasionally rarely never

D READING AND SPEAKING

What do other business people do after work or at the weekend? These are the results of a survey of European senior managers.

GOLFERS

IRELAND	41%
BRITAIN	29%
SWEDEN	26%
GERMANY	5%
ITALY	2%
GREECE	1%

JOGGERS

FINLAND	65%
NORWAY	51%
SWEDEN	41%
ITALY	11%
SPAIN	10%
PORTUGAL	9%

BUSINESS AND LEISURE ACTIVITIES*

SOCIALIZE WITH FRIENDS	59%
LISTEN TO/PLAY CLASSICAL MUSIC	41%
READ BOOKS FOR PLEASURE	41%
WORK ON A COMPUTER AT HOME	24%
ENTERTAIN BUSINESS CONTACTS	24%

*At least once a week

SOURCE: *The European*: 15-18 October 1992 "Lifestyle" survey

1 What differences are there between the north and south of Europe? Why is there a difference?

2 Is your country on the charts? What are the most popular sports and leisure activities for business and professional people in your country?

E

PAIR WORK

Person A: Your information is in File B, page 156.

Person B: You are staying in England for one month. You want to join the local tennis club. Phone the club and ask for information.
— far from the town centre?
— bus from the town centre?
— expensive?
— bar?
— many members?

Start like this:
Good morning. I'd like some information about your tennis club.

F

PRACTICE

1 Ask your partner about their leisure activities. Find out what they do, then ask for more details. The first one is done for you.

a	Go jogging? *Do you go jogging?*	When? How many kilometres? *When do you go?* *How many kilometres do you go?*
b	Play golf?	When? Where? How often?
c	Socialize with friends?	Where? At home? At their home? What / do?
d	Listen to music?	What music / listen? When?
e	Read books?	What? When?
f	Work on a computer?	For business? For pleasure?
g	Entertain business contacts?	At home? In restaurants? How often?

2 Now tell the class about your partner.

He goes jogging at weekends. He jogs five kilometres.

G

VOCABULARY

We *go* jogging (or *jog*), but we *play* golf, and we *do* gymnastics.

1 Look at the list of activities. Do we use *go*, *play*, or *do*?

swimming	cycling	squash	riding
football	running	aerobics	volleyball
tennis	judo	skiing	a sport

2 Which of these sports do you do? Write your answers like this.

I go jogging. I don't play golf.

2

Preparing a trip

2.1 Choosing a hotel

Question forms

Is there... ?   Are there... ?   How many... ?

A SPEAKING

Discuss the following questions in pairs or groups.

a Why do people visit your country: for business, pleasure, or both?
b Where do business people stay when they visit your country?
c What kind of hotels are there?
d Are hotels in your country expensive?
e What is important when you choose a hotel?
f You are travelling to New York on business. What questions do you ask the travel agent?

B LISTENING

Isabelle Dussart is a publisher. She works in London for Hachette, the French publishing company. Next month, she has a meeting in New York. She doesn't know New York, so she asks an American colleague, Larry, about it.

1 Listen to the conversation. Are these statements true (T) or false (F)? Tick the boxes.

		T	F
a	Her budget is $150 a day.	☐	☐
b	She is staying for three days.	☐	☐
c	Rockefeller Center is an arts centre.	☐	☐
d	There are a lot of good restaurants in New York.	☐	☐
e	Isabelle likes swimming.	☐	☐
f	Central Park is dangerous.	☐	☐

2 Now listen again and check your answers. Fill in the spaces.

a .... hotels in that part of town?
b .... some great restaurants in New York and .... usually a ballet at the Lincoln Center.
c ○ Where can I find a list of hotels? .... a guide?
● .... several.
d .... lots of yellow cabs.

LANGUAGE NOTE

There is... / There are...

Singular

Is there a swimming-pool in the hotel?	*Yes, there is.*
	No, there isn't.

Plural

Are there any art galleries near the hotel?	*Yes, there are.*
	No, there aren't.
How many rooms are there in the hotel?	*There are two hundred.*

C

READING

Larry gives Isabelle a guide to hotels in New York.

1 Match the symbols (1–6), the facilities (a–f), and the definitions (A–F), (e.g. **1–c–F**).

1 

2 

3 

4 

5 

6 

a swimming-pool
b business centre
c airport shuttle
d car park
e express checkout
f exercise facility

A a room equipped with PCs, faxes, etc.
B a place to swim
C a place to leave your car
D a place to work out; a gym
E a way of paying your bill early
F a private bus to the airport

2 Read the extract below and find the information.

NEW YORK HOTEL GUIDE

RADISSON EMPIRE HOTEL
44 West 63rd Street
New York, NY 10023
Phone: 212-265-7400
Fax: 212-315-0349

Hotel Overview: Moderate Hotel, 30 minutes from LaGuardia Airport
Restaurant: *The Empire Grill*: B/L/D

SWISSOTEL NEW YORK (THE DRAKE)
440 Park Avenue
at 56th Street
New York, NY 10022
Phone: 212-421-0900
Fax: 212-371-4190

Hotel Overview: Business Hotel, 9 miles from LaGuardia Airport
Restaurant: *Cafe Swiss*: B/L, Drake Bar: B/L/D

THE WALDORF-ASTORIA
301 Park Avenue
New York, NY 10022
Phone: 212-355-3000
Fax: 212-421-8103

Hotel Overview: Deluxe Hotel, 15 miles from LaGuardia Airport
Restaurant: *Peacock Alley*: B/L/D; *Bowl & Bale*: L/D; Oscar's: B/L/D; *Inaglku*: L/D

LOEWS NEW YORK HOTEL
569 Lexington Avenue
New York, NY 10022
Phone: 212-752-7000
Fax: 212-758-6311

Hotel Overview: Moderate Hotel, 8 miles from LaGuardia Airport
Restaurant: *Lexington Avenue Grille*: B/L/D

THE PLAZA HOTEL
5th Avenue
at 59th Street
New York, NY 10019
Phone: 212-759-3000
Fax: 212-759-3167

Hotel Overview: Deluxe Hotel, 10 miles from LaGuardia Airport
Restaurant: *Edwardian Room*: B/L/D; *Palm Court*: B/L/D; *Oyster Bar*: L/D; *Oak Room*: L/D; *Plaza Lounge*: D

a What is the phone number for Loews New York Hotel?
b Is there a gym at the Waldorf Astoria?
c Which hotels have pools?
d Which two hotels are the most expensive?

3 Look at the map and find the hotels in the Guide (A-E). Which hotel is close to the Rockefeller Center?

4 Which is the best hotel for Isabelle? Think about the following before you answer:

- What is her budget?
- Where is her meeting?
- What does she want to do in her free time?

(Look at the tapescript for B if necessary)

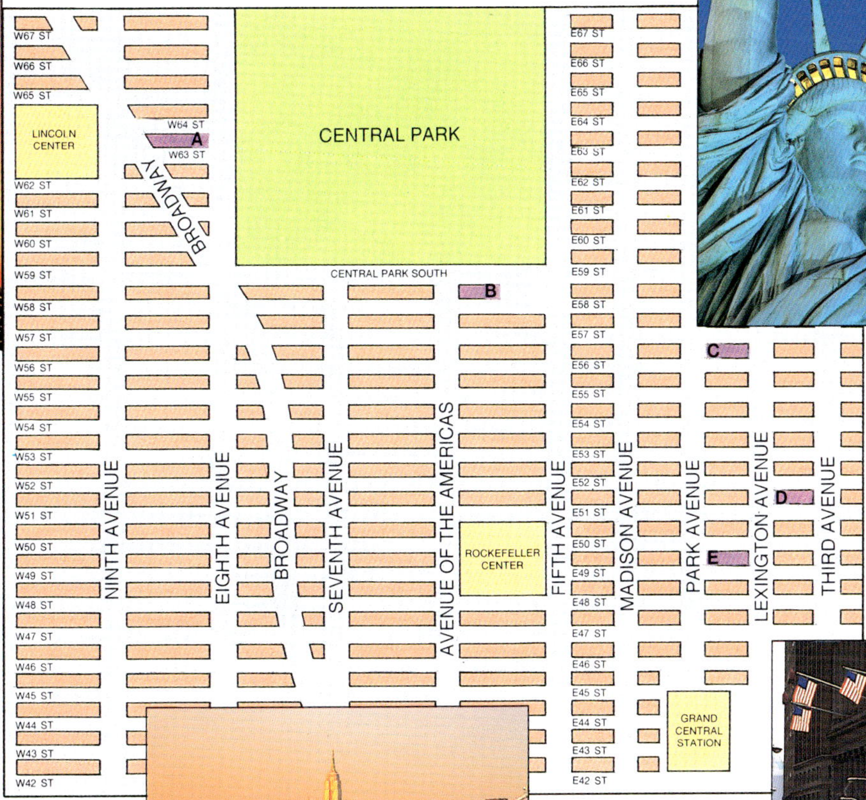

LANGUAGE FOCUS

1 Here are some questions and answers about the Waldorf Astoria Hotel. Use the hotel information on page 26 to fill in the spaces.

a	Is there a gymnasium?	Yes, there is.
b	Is there a swimming-pool?	....
c	.... garage?	....
d	.... Airport Shuttle?	....
e	How many .... ?	Four, but only two do breakfast.
f	.... ?	Yes. The number's 212 421 8103.

2 Now make more questions about the other hotels and ask your partner:
Is there… ? *Are there… ?* *How many… ?*

3 Imagine you are going to New York next month. Which hotel do you want to stay at? Why?

2.2 Booking a hotel

Making requests

Can I... ? Could you... ?

SEE LANGUAGE FILES: 9, 18

A LISTENING

Isabelle Dussart phones the Radisson Empire Hotel to reserve a room.

1 Before you listen, match the questions with the answers.

1 Could I have your name, please ?
2 Could you send me a fax to confirm?
3 Could you spell that?
4 Can you give me your fax number?
5 Can you hold the line?

a Yes. It's 315 0349.
b Dussart.
c OK.
d Of course. What's your number?
e D-U-S-S-A-R-T.

2 Listen and write down the information that Isabelle gives the receptionist.

RADISSON EMPIRE HOTEL
BOOKING FORM

Name: ....

Room: Single/Double

Dates: From:.......................To:...............................

Price: $.............

3 Listen again and fill in the spaces.

a ○ Good morning, Radisson Empire. .... help you?
● Yes, ... to book a room, please.

b ○ .... your name, please?
● Dussart. Isabelle Dussart.
○ .... name, please?
● D-U-S-S-A-R-T.

c ○ .... a fax to confirm your booking ?
● Of course. .... your fax number?

B

PRACTICE

1 Choose which responses (a – d) are correct. Sometimes more than one answer is possible. Are any of the answers impolite?

1 Could I use your fax?
a Yes, of course. c No, thanks.
b Yes, I can. d I'm sorry, it's out of order.

2 Could you help me?
a I'm afraid I can't. c Yes, please.
b Yes, certainly. d No, I can't.

3 Can I leave early today?
a I'm afraid not. c Not at all.
b I'm sorry. We're too busy. d Yes, thank you.

4 Could you lend me your calculator?
a Yes. Here you are. c Not at all.
b Yes, of course. d I'm afraid I can't. It's broken.

5 May I open the window?
a No, don't. c Yes, go ahead.
b Sorry. d I'd rather you didn't.

2 Now look at the Language Note and check your answers.

LANGUAGE NOTE

Making requests

You want to do something	Positive Responses	Negative Responses
Can I … ?	*Certainly.*	*I'm sorry...*
Could I … ?	*Yes, of course.*	*I'm afraid not.*
May I… ?	*Yes, go ahead.*	*I'd rather you didn't.*

You want someone to do something	Positive Responses	Negative Responses
Could you ... ?	*Certainly.*	*I'm afraid I can't.*
Can you ... ?	*Yes, of course.*	

Notice the polite expressions used for negative responses: *I'm sorry..., I'm afraid..., I'd rather...* . Direct expressions like *No, don't* and *No, you can't* sound impolite.

C PRACTICE

In pairs, practise asking and answering the questions. Use the verb in brackets, like this:

In a restaurant, you want the menu. (bring)

○ *Could you bring me the menu, please?*

● *Yes, of course. Here you are.*

1 In a restaurant, you want some water. (have)
2 You want to leave a meeting early. (leave)
3 You want to use a colleague's dictionary. (lend)
4 You want to smoke. (smoke)
5 You want to know the time. (tell)
6 You want to use someone's phone. (use)
7 You want your secretary to type a letter. (type)
8 At work, you want a coffee. (get)

D SPEAKING

The Language Note gives examples of polite expressions used in British English.

Could you ... ? *I'm sorry...*
I'm afraid...

1 What polite expressions do you use in your language?

2 When do you use them? (With waiters in restaurants? With colleagues at work? With friends?) Think about the situations in C.

3 When do you not use them?

E

PAIR WORK

Person A: Your information is in File C page 157.
Person B: Telephone the Plaza Hotel (Person A) and book a double room for yourself.

Your name:	Hans Loeffner
Dates:	From April 23rd to 25th.
Check the price:	*How much... ?*
Check the fax number:	*Could you... ?*

F

WRITING

Isabelle sends a fax to confirm her booking. These are the details she needs to confirm.

Dates: *8 – 11 March*
Type of room: *Single with bath*
Price: *$165 per night*
Time of arrival at hotel: *about 9 p.m.*

1 Fill in the spaces in the fax.

FROM HACHETTE (LONDON) FEB. 3 1995 02:26PM P01

FAX

Attention: Reservations
Radisson Empire Hotel,
New York
From: Isabelle Dussart, Hachette (London) 3/2/95

Dear Sirs,

This fax is to confirm my .... (1) at your hotel for three .... (2) from .... (3) to .... (4), at a .... (5) of .... (6) per night.

I would like a .... (7) room with .... (8) .

I expect to .... (9) at the hotel at about .... (10) o'clock.

Yours faithfully

Isabelle Dussart
Isabelle Dussart

2 Later, Isabelle decides to stay an extra night. Write another fax to the hotel to ask if this is possible.

2.3 Flying out

Telling the time

a quarter past six *6.15 p.m.* *18.15*

A SPEAKING

1 What time do you do these things? Fill in the table below with a partner.

	You	Your partner
start work/college	....	....
finish work/college	....	....
have dinner at home	....	....
go out for dinner	....	....
watch TV	....	....
watch the news on TV	....	....
go shopping	....	....
go to bed	....	....

2 Now discuss your answers with the rest of the class. Do any of the answers surprise you?

3 Do people do these things at different times in other countries?

B READING

Read this extract from a guide to New York.

Opening and Closing Times

New York is a 24-hour-a-day city. The subways and buses run round the clock and plenty of services are available 24 hours a day, seven days a week.

Banks are open from 9-3 from Monday to Friday, with certain branches open late on Friday.

Post offices are open weekdays from 10 to 5. The main post office on Eighth Avenue is open 24 hours a day.

Museums are closed on Mondays, but open late on Tuesdays or Thursdays.

Stores are usually open 10-5 Monday-Saturday. In residential neighbourhoods, stores are open later and they are also open on Sundays.

1 Answer these questions.

a How long are banks open for?
b What time do banks open?

2 Here are some answers. What are the questions? The first one is done for you.

a	*When do banks close?*	3 p.m.
b		On Mondays.
c		10 a.m.
d		Friday.
e		5 o'clock.
f		Every day of the week.

LANGUAGE NOTE

Telling the time

1 In conversation, we use *past* (Am. English: *after*) and *to* (Am. English: *of*).
5.20 *twenty past five* (Am. English: *twenty after five*)
5.50 *ten to six* (Am. English: *ten of six*)

For 30 minutes past the hour, we say *half past.*
5.30 *half past five*

For 15 and 45 minutes, we use *a quarter.*
5.15 *a quarter past five* (Am. English: *a quarter after five*)
5.45 *a quarter to six* (Am. English: *a quarter of six)*

2 More formally, we use figures only (without *past* and *to, half* and *quarter*).
5.05 *five oh five*
5.15 *five fifteen*
5.20 *five twenty*
5.45 *five forty-five*
5.50 *five fifty*

With this 12-hour form, we use *a.m.* for morning and *p.m.* for afternoon.
Breakfast is served between 7.00 a.m. and 9.00 a.m.
The office closes at 5.30 p.m.

3 For itineraries and timetables, we often use the 24-hour clock.
5.20 p.m. = 17.20 (*seventeen twenty*)
5.45 a.m. = 05.45 (*five forty-five*)

C LANGUAGE FOCUS

1 Look at the pictures. What time is it?

a

b

c

2 Study the table below and complete it.

STANDARD		24-HOUR CLOCK (itineraries, timetables, etc.)	
three o'clock	three	fifteen hundred (hours)	15.00
five past three	three oh five	fifteen oh five	15.05
quarter past three	....	fifteen fifteen	15.15
....	....	....	15.25
half past three	three thirty	....	15.30
twenty-five to four	....	fifteen thirty-five	15.35
....	three forty-five	....	15.45
....	....	....	15.55

D ROLE PLAY

Person A: Turn to File D page 157.

Person B: You are Isabelle Dussart. You go to the travel agent to get information on flights to New York. You want to arrive on Tuesday evening. Your meeting is on Wednesday at 10 a.m.

Find out the information you need. Ask questions based on the notes below.

— How long / take / London to New York?
How long does it take to fly from London to New York?

— How much / cost?
— What / time difference between London and New York?
— How many flights / per day?
— / afternoon flight?
— What time / arrive?

E

LISTENING

Isabelle Dussart is waiting for her plane. Listen and complete the missing details.

TIME	DESTINATION	FLIGHT NO.	INFORMATION	GATE NO.
....	ATHENS	BA 651	BOARDING	....
12.30	NEW YORK	....	BOARDING	51
....	STOCKHOLM	SK 444	BOARDING	....
....	....	IB 414	BOARDING	40
....	....	JL 519	DELAYED	–
....	....	....	DELAYED UNTIL 15.00	16

F

PRACTICE

Time Bingo

Work in groups of three or four.

Person A: You call the list of times below to the other players. Read the numbers in the order they appear.

Person B/C/D: Choose one of the bingo cards at the back of the book and follow the instructions. (**Person B:** File E, page 157; **Person C:** File I, page 158; **Person D:** File O, page 161).

09.25	02.00	06.05
17.50	11.45	19.10
18.45	13.05	10.55
04.55	07.30	22.20
15.10	12.30	14.15
10.00	16.10	12.15
09.40	20.00	08.45
07.20	23.35	11.15
05.05	03.40	21.30

3

Away on business

3.1 Arriving

Countable and uncountable nouns

How much... ? *How many... ?*

SEE LANGUAGE FILES: 4

A **SPEAKING**

Here is a list of ten things people often take when they go away on business.

electric shaver
book to read on the plane
food from home
adaptor plug
phrasebook
indigestion tablets
Walkman
extra pair of shoes
first-aid kit
gift for host/colleagues

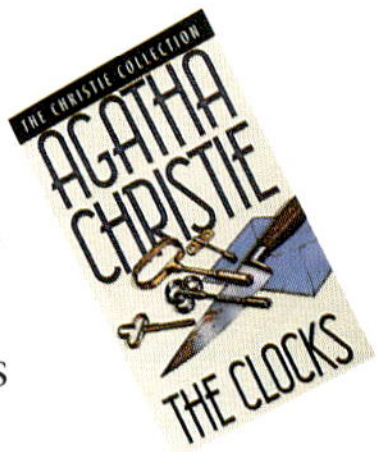

You and your partner are going on a business trip. You can only take five of the ten items. Decide which items to take and which to leave behind.

B **LISTENING**

Robert Dillon is an accountant. He works for KPMG in New York. He is in England on business. He arrives at Heathrow Airport and travels by train and then taxi to his hotel in Oxford.

1 Listen to the four dialogues. Where is he in each dialogue?

2 Listen again and answer the questions.

a How long is he staying?
b How many bags has he got?
c How much money does he change?
d How much does the taxi cost?

LANGUAGE NOTE

Countable and uncountable nouns

1 Countable nouns have a plural form. To ask a question about quantity, we use *How many... ?*
How many bags have you got?
How many appointments have you got today?

2 Uncountable nouns have no plural form. To ask a question about quantity, we use *How much... ?*
How much luggage have you got ?
How much money have you got?
How much wine do you have with your dinner?

LANGUAGE FOCUS

1 Are these words countable or uncountable? Mark them C or U.

paper	people	sugar
days	meat	rooms

2 Fill in the spaces in the questions below. Use *How many... ?*, *How much ... ?*, and the words in **1** above. The first one is done for you.

1 *How* *many* *people* work in your head office?
2 .... are there in this hotel?
3 .... do you take in your coffee?
4 .... do you eat in a week?
5 .... is the company closed for New Year?
6 .... is there in the photocopier?

3 Now match the questions in **2** with the replies below. The first one is done for you.

a Two spoonfuls, please. *3*
b Only three more sheets. Could you fill it, please?
c None. I'm a vegetarian.
d About two hundred, with another five hundred in our subsidiaries.
e Three hundred. Two hundred double and one hundred single.
f Six, including Christmas Day and New Year's Day.

D

LISTENING

Robert Dillon arrives at The Randolph, a hotel in Oxford.

Listen to the dialogue and complete his registration card.

The Randolph

Room number

Guest Registration Card

Name:	Company:
Nationality:	Number of nights:
Address:	Morning call:
	Payment: [AE/Visa/Diners/Other]

E

ROLE PLAY

Person A: Your information is in File F, page 157.

Person B: You are the receptionist. Check in Person A.
Find out the following information:

— name
— nationality
— company
— number of nights
— method of payment
— morning call? when?

F

READING

Here are five conversations heard in the hotel.

Put the lines of each dialogue in the right order.

1 a Right, Mr Thomson. Here is your key. Room 615.
b Good evening, I've got a reservation.
c Thank you very much.
d Thomson. Richard Thomson.
e What is your name, sir?

2 a Where to, sir?
b Hello, Reception.
c OK, sir. At the front door in five minutes.
d Good evening. I'd like a taxi, please.
e The station, for a train at 7.30.

3 a That's £3.50, please.
b 615. Mr Thomson.
c Gin and tonic, please.
d Certainly, sir. What room is it?
e Could you put it on my bill, please?

4 a Of course, Mrs Jones. Something to drink with it?
b This is Mrs Jones in 543. Could I have a chicken sandwich, please?
c Hello, Room Service.
d Right. Ready in about fifteen minutes, Mrs Jones.
e Yes, please, a bottle of mineral water.

5 a Of course, Madam. What room number?
b Certainly.
c I'd like to check out, please.
d Did you use the mini-bar?
e That's £128.
f Can I pay by cheque?
g No.
h 543.

3.2 Going out

Suggesting, accepting, and refusing

Shall we... ?   *Would you like to... ?*

SEE LANGUAGE FILE: 8

A LISTENING

Robert Dillon telephones a colleague in London from his hotel room.

1 Read the conversation and try to fill in the spaces.

○ Hello. Charles Mant's office.
● Hello. .... Mr Mant, please?
○ I'm sorry, he's out. .... a message?
● Yes. Could you tell him Mr Dillon from KPMG called?
○ .... , please?
● It's an Oxford number. My hotel number is 01865-247481. Can .... today?
○ Yes. He'll be back soon. I'll ask him to call you.
● ....
○ Thank you. Bye.

2 Now listen and check your answers.

PRACTICE

Read this conversation. Use some of the language in A to make it more polite.

○ Yes?
Hello. Mr Walton's office.
● I want to speak to Mr Walton.
Could I speak to Mr Walton, please?
○ He's out. What do you want?
● Tell him I called.
○ Who are you?
● Charmer.
○ Repeat!
● CHARMER.
○ Spell it!
● C-H-A-R-M-E-R.
○ OK.
● Bye.

C ROLE PLAY

In pairs, practise this telephone situation.

Person A (You are John Langford)	Person B (You are Dr Muller's colleague, Dr Heath)
You want to talk to Dr Peter Muller. *Can I speak to Dr Muller, please?*	
	He's not here — give reason. *I'm sorry, ...*
Ask to leave a message.	
	Answer.
Message is: 'Please call John Langford back today.'	
	Check spelling of name.
Spell name.	
	Ask for telephone number.
Give number (0892-824561).	
	Check number.
End call.	
	End call.

LANGUAGE NOTE

Suggesting, accepting, and refusing

1 **Making suggestions**
Shall we... ?
Would you like to... ?
Let's...

2 **Polite replies**
That sounds great!
Sure! (American English)
Good idea!
I'd love to! (British English)

3 **Polite refusals**
I'm afraid I'm not free.
I'm sorry, I can't make it this evening.

D

LISTENING

Charles Mant calls Robert Dillon back.

1 Listen to the conversation and answer the questions.

a When do they decide to meet?
b What is the name of the show?
c What time does it start?
d Where do they agree to meet?

2 Now listen again and answer the questions.

a Robert suggests a meeting. What does he say?
.... *meet one evening?*
b Charles invites Robert. What does he say?
What shall we do? .... *go to the theatre?*
c Charles suggests a place to meet. What does he say?
.... *meet at a restaurant near the theatre.*

E

LANGUAGE FOCUS

You are arranging an evening out.

1 Write some suggestions. Choose things that you like to do.
Would you like to go out for an Indian meal this evening?

2 Now work with a partner. Make your suggestions to your partner and reply to your partner's suggestions.

If you want to accept, remember to be enthusiastic. If you don't like your partner's idea, be polite and make an excuse or another suggestion.
Good idea!
I'm afraid I can't make it this evening.
I'm sorry, but I don't like Indian food. Do you like Chinese food?

F

SPEAKING

In your country, how do business people entertain visitors from abroad? Is it different in other countries?

3.3 Arranging to meet

Giving directions

It's opposite... *Go past...* *Turn left...*

SEE LANGUAGE FILES: 19, 20

A PAIRWORK

Robert Dillon is planning his evening in town. He goes down to Reception to find out about trains to London.

Person A: Your information is in File G on page 158.

Person B: You are Robert Dillon. You want to go to London this evening to see the musical Sunset Boulevard. You want to return to Oxford the same evening. Is this possible? You know the musical starts at 7.45.

Prepare some questions to ask the hotel receptionist (Person A). Two of them are done for you.

— What train / I take?	*What train do I take?*
— What time / show finish?	
— How far / theatre / station?	
— / late train to Oxford?	*Is there a late train to Oxford?*
— What time / it leave London?	
— What time / arrive in Oxford?	
— / taxi service in Oxford at night?	

LANGUAGE NOTE

Giving directions

Here are some useful phrases for giving directions.

Prepositions				Directions
	location		movement	
It's	*next to*	Go	*past*	*Take the first left/right*
	near		*around*	*Go as far as...*
	opposite/facing		*along*	*Go straight on (until...)*
	on the right/left		*up/down*	*Turn left/right (at...)*
	on the corner		*over*	

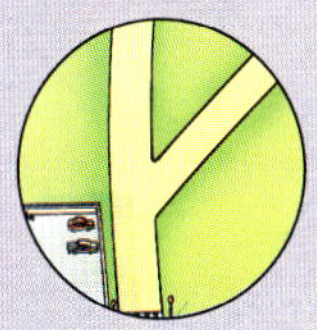
junction

crossroads

roundabout

crossing

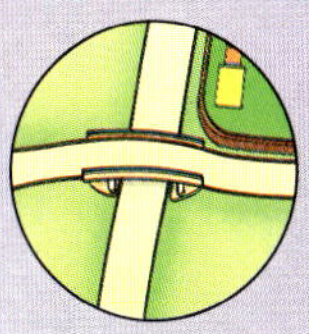
bridge

B

PRACTICE

Answer these questions based on the map. You are at the station.

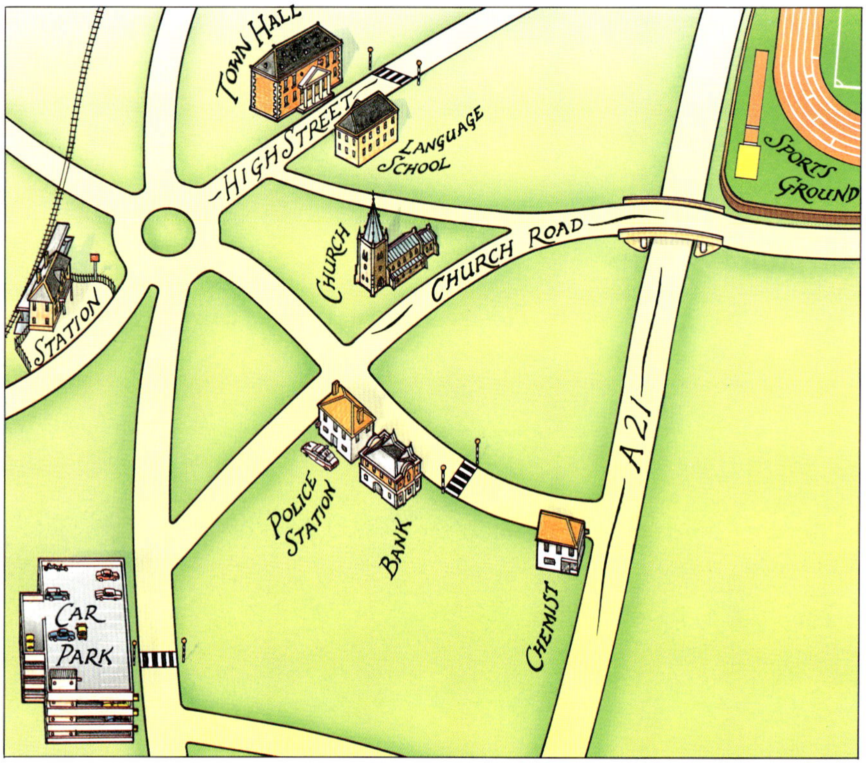

1 Excuse me. How do I get to the church?
2 Excuse me. Can you tell me how to get to the bank?
3 Where's the police station?
4 I'm looking for Church Road.
5 I need to buy some aspirin. Is there a chemist near here?
6 Excuse me. Where is the Town Hall?

C

LISTENING

Robert phones Charles Mant.

Look at the map of London on page 45 and listen to the conversation. Which restaurant do they choose? Find it on the map. What number is it?

D

PAIR WORK

Person A: Your information is in File H on page 158.

Person B:

1 You are at Charing Cross Station. You want to go to the Prince of Wales Theatre. Ask Person A for directions.

2 Now use the map of London to give Person A directions.

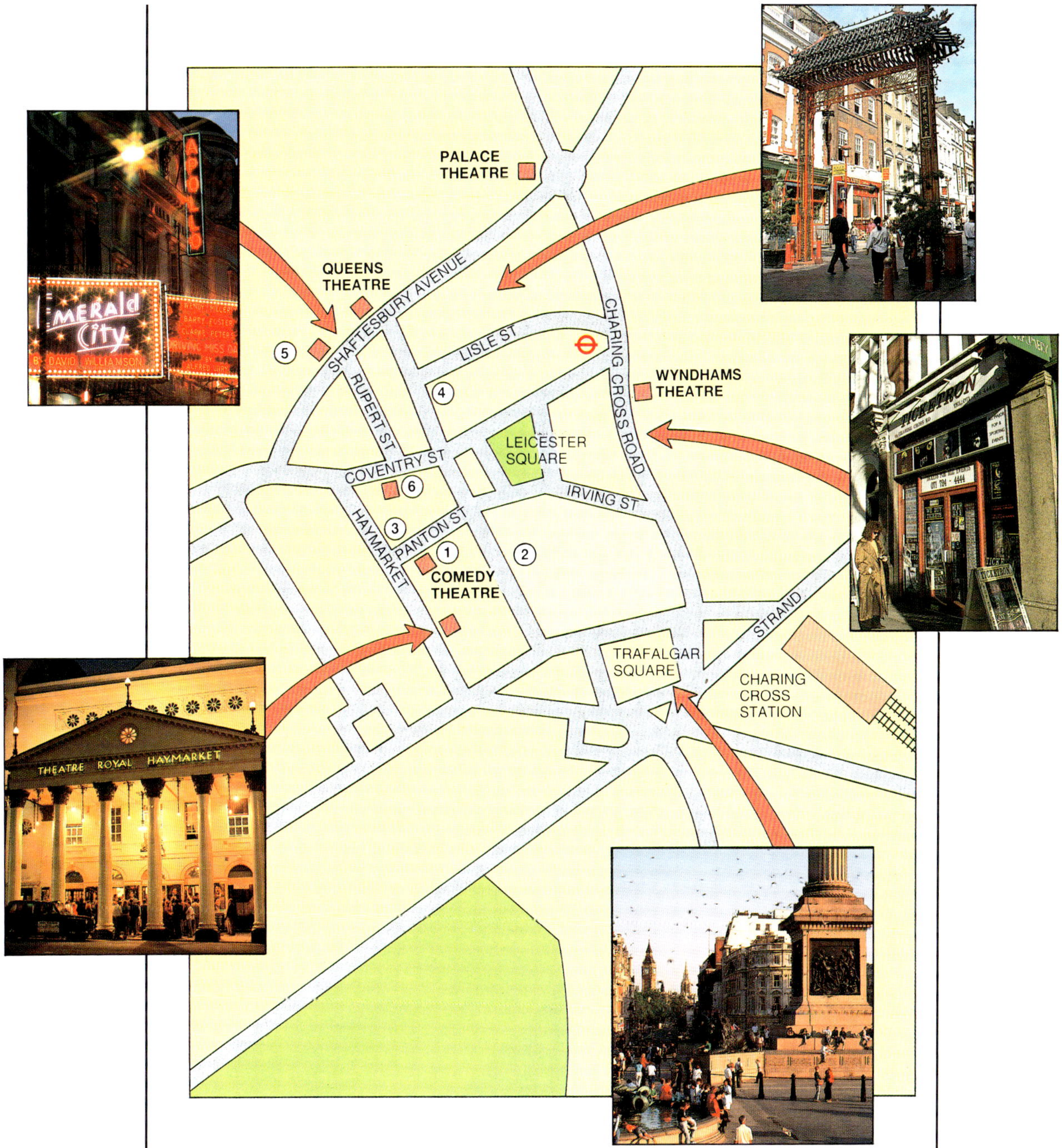

E WRITING

Write a note for a visitor from overseas to explain the way to your office, school, or home from the airport. If you draw a map, write directions in words as well.

3.4 Eating out

Restaurant vocabulary

I'd like... *I recommend...*

A SPEAKING

1. Where can you eat out in your country?
2. What kinds of food can you eat quickly?
3. How long do you take for lunch?

B LISTENING AND PRACTICE

Robert Dillon and Charles Mant go to a wine bar. Charles's wife Sally meets them there.

1 Listen. What do they order?

2 You and your partner are in the wine bar. Look at the menu on page 46 and discuss what you want to eat. Use some of the expressions from the Language Note below.

LANGUAGE NOTE

Restaurant language

Asking for information
What would you like?
What do you want?
What do you recommend?
What exactly is that?

Giving advice
I suggest...
I recommend...

It's a local dish.
It's made of...
It's very spicy.

Ordering
To start.../as a starter...
To follow.../as a main course...
For dessert...

I'd like...
I'll have...

Complaining
Excuse me...

I think this bill is wrong.
That's not what I ordered.
Can you change it?

Paying
Do you take (Visa cards)?

Shall we split the bill?

I'm paying.
Please, I insist.

Is service included?
Can I have a receipt, please?

C VOCABULARY

1 Are these words countable or uncountable? Mark them C or U.

butter	bread	fruit	bottle of wine
water	sugar	mushroom	wine
glass	serviette	salt	soup
glass of water	spoon	pepper	cup of coffee

2 Now ask the waiter for them, like this.

Can I have some bread, please?
Could you bring me a glass of water, please?
I'd like a glass of water, please.

3 Here are some restaurant complaints. Fill in the spaces with one of the words below.

clean cold some hot cup rare stale dirty strong broken

a This soup is .... and I like my soup very .... Can you change it, please?
b This knife is .... Can you bring me a .... one, please?
c This glass is .... Can you bring me another one, please?
d This bread is .... Can you bring me .... fresh bread, please?
e This coffee is very weak and I like .... coffee. Can you bring me another .... , please?
f This steak is very well done, but I asked for .... Can I have another one, please?

D

LISTENING

1 It is the end of the meal. What do you think Charles says in these situations?

a He wants the bill.
b He wants to pay for everyone.
c He wants to pay by American Express.
d He wants a receipt.

2 Now listen and check your answers.

E

SPEAKING

The Restaurant Game

Play the game in groups of three. Choose one of the restaurants opposite.

The aim of the game is to get from the start of the meal to the end as quickly as possible. Throw a coin to see where you land. If it is heads, you move **one** square forward. If it is tails, you move **two** squares forward. To finish, you must land **exactly** on the END square. When you use the right language for the square you land on, you can throw again. If you don't know what to say, you miss a turn!

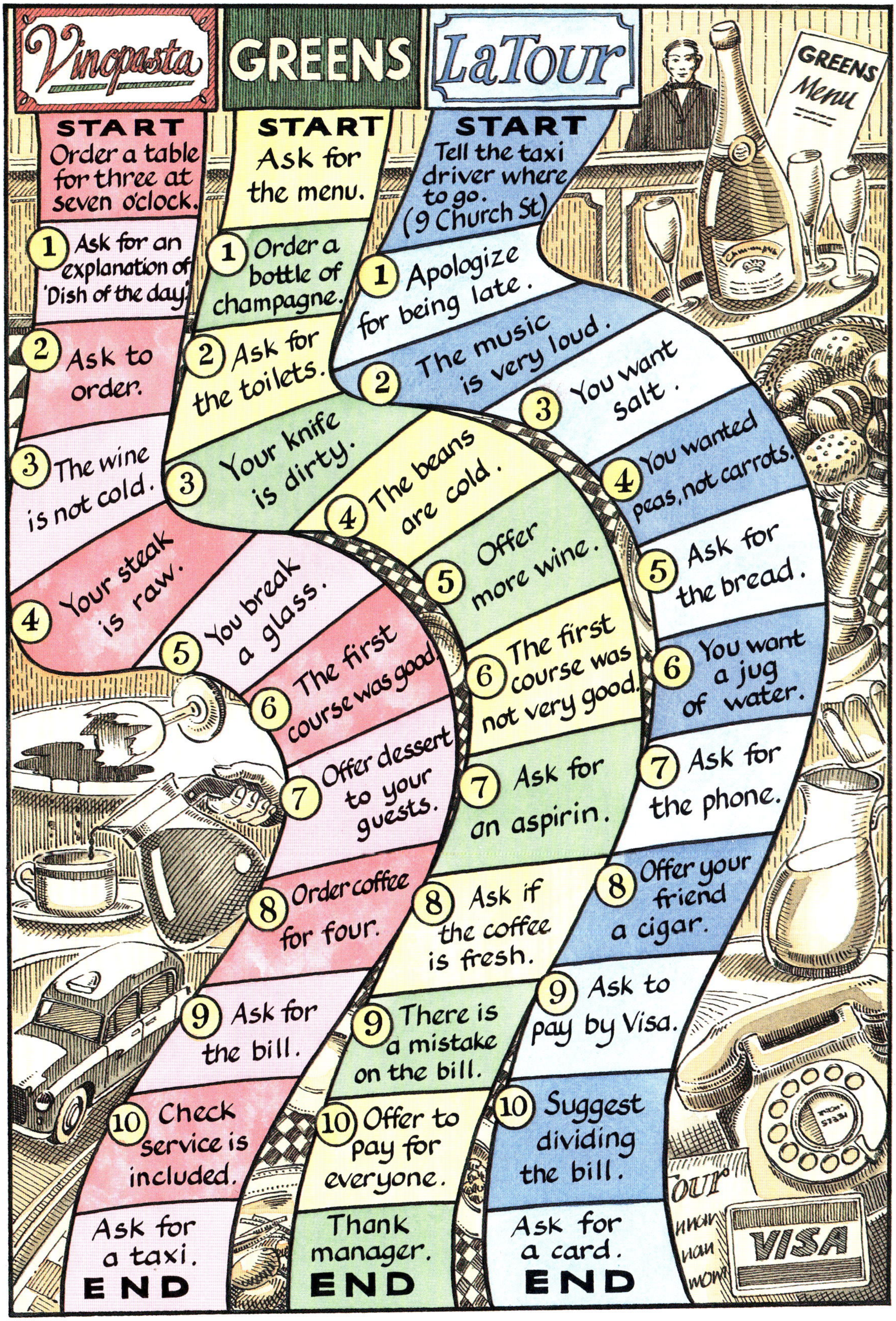
Vinopasta
GREENS
LaTour
START
Order a table for three at seven o'clock.
1 Ask for an explanation of 'Dish of the day'.
2 Ask to order.
3 The wine is not cold.
4 Your steak is raw.
5 You break a glass.
6 The first course was good.
7 Offer dessert to your guests.
8 Order coffee for four.
9 Ask for the bill.
10 Check service is included.
Ask for a taxi.
END
START
Ask for the menu.
1 Order a bottle of champagne.
2 Ask for the toilets.
3 Your knife is dirty.
4 The beans are cold.
5 Offer more wine.
6 The first course was not very good.
7 Ask for an aspirin.
8 Ask if the coffee is fresh.
9 There is a mistake on the bill.
10 Offer to pay for everyone.
Thank manager.
END
START
Tell the taxi driver where to go. (9 Church St)
1 Apologize for being late.
2 The music is very loud.
3 You want salt.
4 You wanted peas, not carrots.
5 Ask for the bread.
6 You want a jug of water.
7 Ask for the phone.
8 Offer your friend a cigar.
9 Ask to pay by Visa.
10 Suggest dividing the bill.
Ask for a card.
END
GREENS Menu
VISA

4

Visiting a company

4.1 Arriving at a company

The Past Simple tense

He went. *He didn't go.* *Did he go?*

SEE LANGUAGE FILES: 3, 7, 14, 15

A

READING

ICL, the British computer company, is a subsidiary of the Japanese firm Fujitsu. The two companies work very closely together.

This is Shigeru Kanemori. He works for Fujitsu in Japan. Last year he visited ICL in England.

1 Here are some documents and receipts from Shigeru Kanemori's first three days in England. What did he do when he was in England?

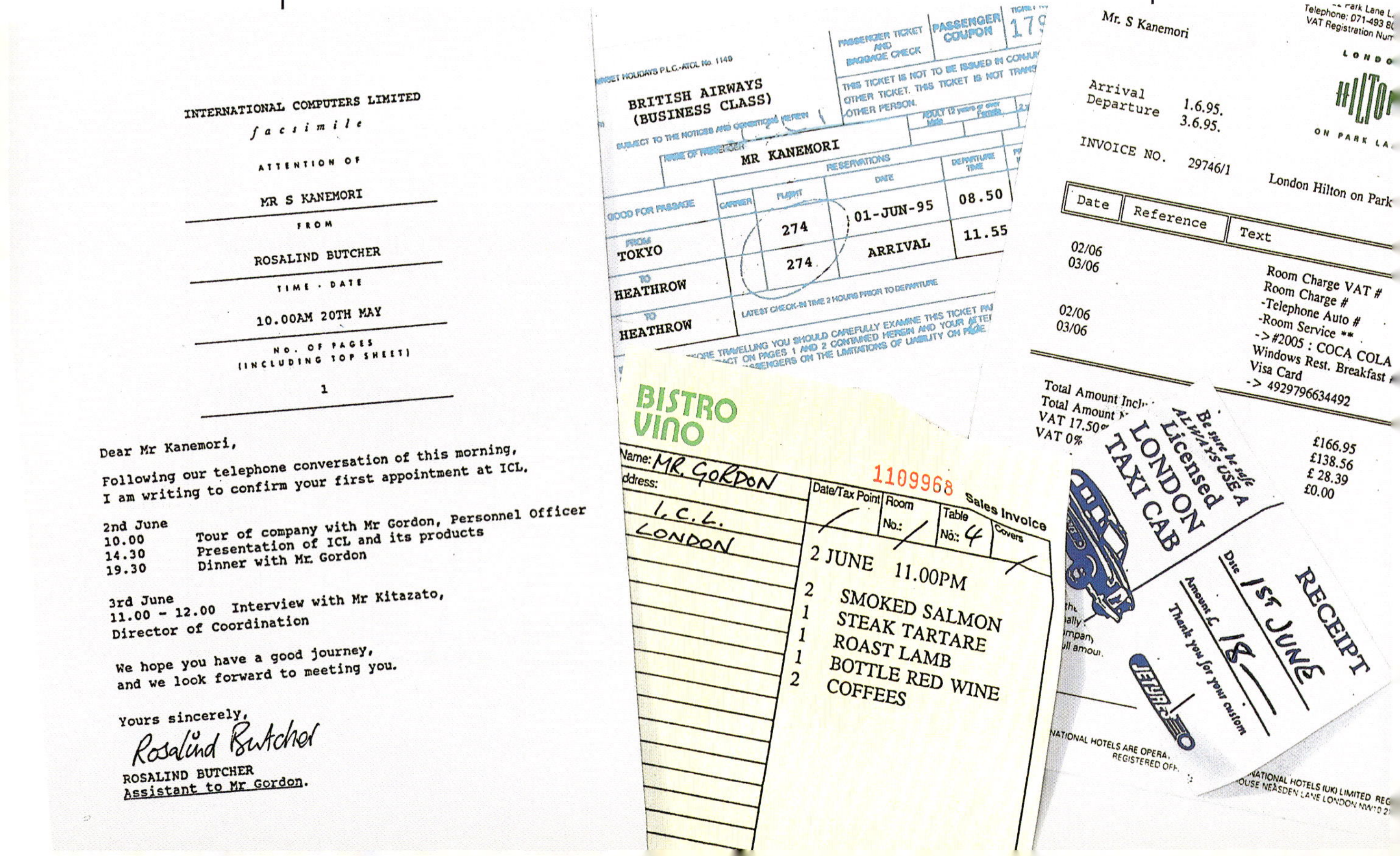

INTERNATIONAL COMPUTERS LIMITED

facsimile

ATTENTION OF

MR S KANEMORI

FROM

ROSALIND BUTCHER

TIME · DATE

10.00AM 20TH MAY

NO. OF PAGES (INCLUDING TOP SHEET)

1

Dear Mr Kanemori,

Following our telephone conversation of this morning, I am writing to confirm your first appointment at ICL.

2nd June
10.00 Tour of company with Mr Gordon, Personnel Officer
14.30 Presentation of ICL and its products
19.30 Dinner with Mr Gordon

3rd June
11.00 - 12.00 Interview with Mr Kitazato, Director of Coordination

We hope you have a good journey, and we look forward to meeting you.

Yours sincerely,

Rosalind Butcher

ROSALIND BUTCHER
Assistant to Mr Gordon.

2 Now answer these questions about Shigeru's trip. Use the Past Simple tense in your answers. The first one is done for you.

Regular verbs (green)	Irregular verbs (blue)
The Past Simple ends in *-ed*	Look at page 172 for the Past Simple form.

a Where did he go? go/fly *He went/flew to Heathrow.*
b When did he leave Tokyo ? leave
c When did he arrive? get to arrive
d How did he travel? travel fly/take
e Where did he stay? stay
f How many nights did he stay there? stay
g What did he do at ICL on 2nd June? attend see visit
h Where did he go in the evening? go
i Who did he have dinner with? have
j What did they eat? have
k Who did he meet on 3rd June? meet
l How did he pay for the hotel? pay

B

QUESTION-MAKING AND PRACTICE

Look again at the information about Shigeru's visit to London.

1 Here are some answers. What are the questions? The first one is done for you.

a	Did *he stay for only one night?*	No, he didn't. He stayed for two nights.
b	What time	At 11.00.
c	What	He attended a presentation at ICL.
d	Who	Mr Gordon.
e	How	By taxi.
f	Where	At the Hilton Hotel.
g	Did	Yes, they did – red wine.

2 Ask your partner about his or her last business trip or holiday.

Where / go?	How / travel?	What / do there?
When / go?	How long / stay?	Who / meet?
When / arrive?	Where / stay?	When / come back?

LANGUAGE NOTE

The Past Simple

We use the Past Simple tense to describe actions in the past.

1 **Regular and irregular**
To put a regular verb into the Past Simple, we add *-ed* (or *-d* if the infinitive ends in *-e*):
play – played   move – *moved*

Many verbs are irregular in the Past Simple. There is a list on pages 172-3.

2 **Questions and negative forms**
In questions, we use the auxiliary *did.*
In the negative form, we use *didn't.*
Where did he eat last Sunday?
Did you go there yesterday?
I didn't attend the presentation.

3 **The verb *to be***
We don't use the auxiliary *did* with the verb *to be.*
*I **wasn't** in Tokyo on 2nd June – I **was** at ICL.*
*Where **were** you?*

C

PRONUNCIATION

The regular past simple ending *-ed* or *-d* has three different pronunciations: /t/, /d/, and /ɪd/.

Listen to the words below and put them in the correct column. The first three are done for you.

opened	smoked	played	visited
worked	returned	repeated	arrived
waited	watched	attended	stopped
finished	stayed	needed	decided

/t/	/d/	/ɪd/
worked	opened	waited

D

READING AND WRITING

At the end of his first day at ICL, Shigeru Kanemori received a fax from a friend in London.

1 Complete the fax, using an appropriate form of the verb in brackets. The first one is done for you.

INDEX ENGINEERING PLC

FAX

Attention of: Shigeru Kanemori c/o Hilton Hotel, London
No. of pages incl. top sheet: 1

From: Peter Wilsdon
Time/Date: 02:00pm 2 June

Please telephone us immediately if you do not receive the number of pages indicated

Dear Shigeru

Welcome to Britain. Did you have (you/have)[1] a good journey? .... (you/be)[2] tired when you .... (get)[3] here? What .... (you/do)[4] last night? I'm sure you .... (not/go)[5] to the night-club!

I .... (come)[6] to your hotel this morning, but you .... (not/be)[7] here. The receptionist .... (tell)[8] me that you .... (leave)[9] the hotel at about 9 a.m. I .... (not/be)[10] surprised because I knew that you have a meeting at ICL today.

If you are free tomorrow, phone me or fax me on 0171-222 1234, and we'll have a drink together.

Best wishes,

Peter

INDEX ENGINEERING PLC INDEX HOUSE BAKER STREET LONDON W1A 1AA Tel. 0171 222 1234

2 Now write a fax from Shigeru to Peter.

a Thank him for his fax.
b Answer his questions in the first paragraph.
c Explain where you were today (meetings at ICL).
d Explain that you are busy this evening and can't meet him for a drink. *I'm afraid....*
e Suggest that you meet tomorrow. *Let's....*

4.2 Meeting new people

Introductions and conversation openers

Welcome to... *Pleased to meet you.*

SEE LANGUAGE FILE: 9

A SPEAKING

1 How do you welcome overseas visitors in your company/country? How is it different in other companies/countries?

2 When you meet a visitor you don't know, do you use their first name:

a straight away?
b after a period of time? (How long?)
c never?

3 Imagine you are a foreign business person, visiting your country for the first time. What are the most surprising / interesting / nice / unpleasant things you would notice?

B READING AND LISTENING

It's Shigeru Kanemori's first day at ICL. He is meeting Mark Gordon, the Personnel Officer.

1 Try to complete Mark Gordon's words.

MG	Mr Kanemori, how do you do? I'm Mark Gordon, Personnel Officer. .... to ICL.
SK	Thank you.
MG	.... a good journey?
SK	Yes, thank you. It was a long flight, but I slept for a few hours.
MG	And .... happy with your hotel?
SK	Yes, it's very comfortable and it's in a good position.
MG	I'm pleased to hear that. .... a coffee before we start?
SK	No, thank you. I had a cup of coffee just now.
MG	So, ... visit to England?
SK	Yes, it is.
MG	Well, I .... a nice stay.
SK	Thank you very much. I'm sure I'll enjoy my visit here.

2 Now listen and check answers.

PRACTICE

Shigeru meets a lot of people on his first day.

1 Look at the pictures, and match sentences 1-6 with letters a-f.

1 How do you do?
2 This is Mr Kanemori. He's from Fujitsu.
3 Can I introduce myself? I'm Mr Kanemori.
4 Can I introduce you to Mr Evans? He works in Accounts.
5 How do you do?
6 Pleased to meet you. I'm Mrs Stevens, Mary Stevens.

2 Imagine you are meeting your colleagues in the class for the first time. Introduce yourself to the person on your right. Then introduce yourselves to another pair.

LANGUAGE NOTE

Introductions

1 **Introducing yourself**
Hello. I'm...
Can I introduce myself?
My name's...
How do you do? I'm...

2 **Introducing another person**
This is...
Can I introduce you to... ?

3 **Responding to an introduction**
How do you do?
Pleased to meet you.
Nice to meet you.

4 **Making a visitor feel at home**
Welcome to... (name of your company)
Did you have a good journey?
Do sit down./ Please take a seat.
Would you like something to eat/drink?
Is this your first visit to... ?
I hope you enjoy your stay.

D **PRACTICE**

You are visiting a company.

1 Your host says sentences a-j below to you. How can you reply? Choose from replies 1-10.

1 Yes, please.
2 It's a pleasure.
3 Yes, of course.
4 It doesn't matter.
5 No, I don't.
6 How do you do?
7 I'm pleased to hear that.
8 Fine, thank you.
9 Thank you.
10 Yes, I did.

2 Can you think of any more replies not on the list?

E

PAIR WORK

Person A is meeting **Person B** at the airport. It is their first meeting. Use the notes below to prepare a conversation. When you reach the end of the notes, try to continue the conversation.

Person A	Person B
Say hello. Introduce yourself.	
	Say hello. Introduce yourself.
Ask B about his/her journey.	
	Answer. Thank A for meeting you.
Answer. Offer to take B's suitcase.	
	Answer.
Ask B if he/she wants to eat something.	
	No. Lunch on plane.
Ask B if this is his/her first visit to your country	
	No. Two weeks last year as a tourist. But this is first business trip.
Reply. *Oh, really? Where?*	
	Answer.

F

LISTEN AND REPLY

You are visiting a client at ICL. While you are sitting in his office, one of his colleagues comes in and starts speaking to you. Listen and reply.

4.3 Explaining company structure

Company organization
division *subsidiary* *parent company*

A

SPEAKING

Many companies are multinational: they operate in several different countries.

1 What advantages and disadvantages do multinational companies have (compared with smaller companies)?

2 Would you prefer to work for a big multinational company, or a small company? Why?

LANGUAGE NOTE

Company structure

*ICL is a **subsidiary** of Fujitsu.*
*Fujitsu is the **parent company** of ICL.*

The group	***consists of***	*twenty-nine companies.*
	is made up of / ***is divided into***	*three divisions.*
	operates in	*six target markets.*

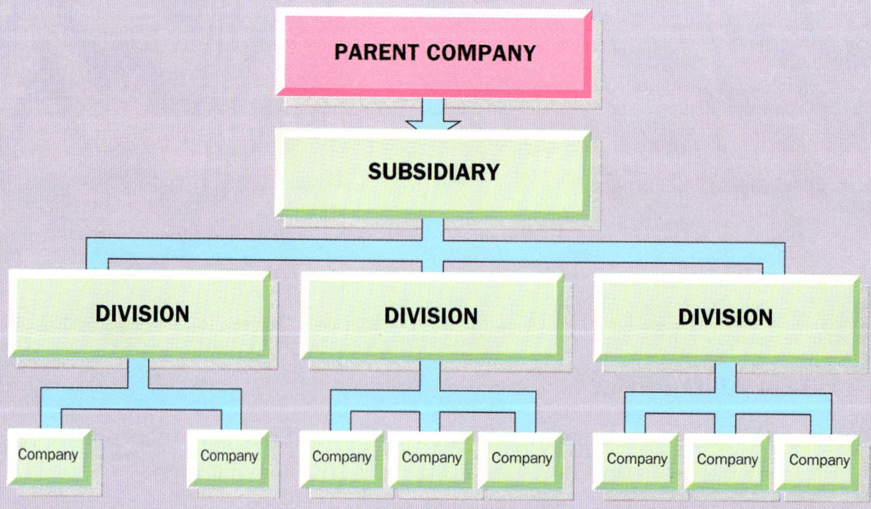

B

LISTENING

Shigeru Kanemori and some colleagues from Japan are attending a presentation of ICL. A senior executive is talking about how the company is organized.

Listen, and complete the chart.

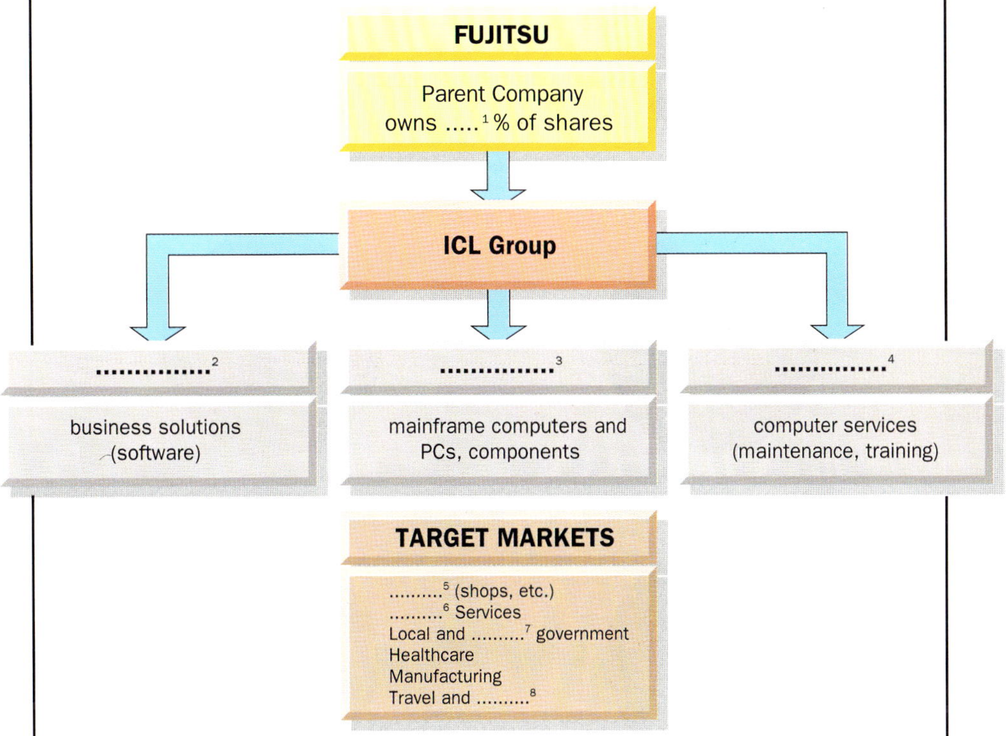

C

LANGUAGE FOCUS

Fill in the spaces using the words below.

divided into	subsidiary	division
retail	manufactures	employs

ICL is a .... (1) of Fujitsu, which is an 82% shareholder in the company. The company .... (2) a total of 24,000 people.

ICL group consists of twenty-nine autonomous companies. Each company has its own Managing Director. The group is .... (3) three divisions. The first is Industry Systems. This division produces business solutions (software) for ICL's customers. The second is Technology, which .... (4) computers and components. The third .... (5) is Services, which sells computer services, like maintenance and training.

ICL operates in six different target markets: .... (6) – that's shops, supermarkets and so on; financial services; local and central government; healthcare; manufacturing; and travel and transport.

D VOCABULARY AND SPEAKING

1 Eight people are describing their job. Match the people (a-h) with the department they work in. The first one is done for you.

a 'We buy raw materials and equipment for the company.'

b 'We help if a client has problems with a product.'

c 'If there is a problem with a contract, we deal with it.'

d 'We recruit and train staff.'

e 'We study and test possible new products.'

f 'We find potential clients for new products and organize advertising campaigns.'

g 'We manufacture the products.'

h 'We sell the products.'

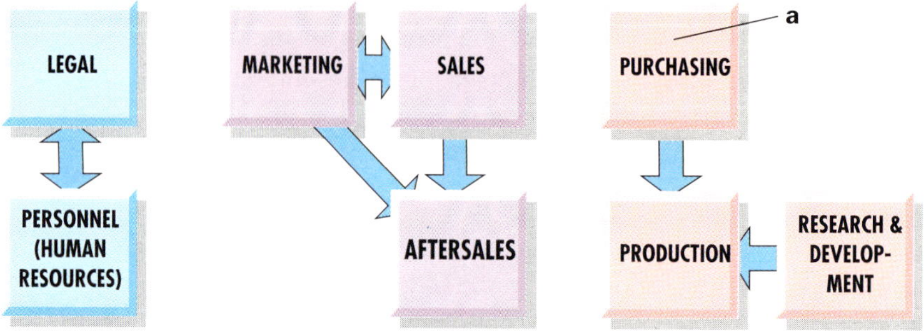

2 Which do you think is the most interesting department to work in? Which is the least interesting? Why?

E

PRONUNCIATION

1 Underline the syllable which has the main stress. The first one is done for you.

pro<u>duc</u>tion	advertise	develop
produce	advertising	development
product	advertisement	recruit
accounts	purchase	recruitment
accountant	purchasing	research

2 Listen and check your answers.

3 Now listen to the words in complete sentences.

a We want more resources for the Research and Development department.
b We plan to recruit new personnel in the Accounts department.
c We are advertising new jobs in the Production department.

4 Write some sentences of your own using the words in the list and read them to your partner. Write down the sentences your partner reads to you.

F

PRACTICE

1 Draw an organization chart for your own company or a company you know.

2 Write a description, using the text in C as a model.

3 Present your company to a colleague, or to the class.

5

New developments

5.1 Current activities

The Present Continuous tense

She's going. *She isn't going.* *Is she going?*

SEE LANGUAGE FILE: 12

A

READING

Linda Dawson is a buyer for Marks & Spencer. She chooses the suppliers for some items which Marks & Spencer sells.

1 Read the article about Linda in the Marks & Spencer in-house magazine and answer the questions.

a What does she like to do in her spare time?
b What are her ambitions for the future?
c What was her previous job?

A DAY IN MY LIFE

I get up at about six and plan my day. I leave the house at 7.00 a.m. and catch the 7.15 to London. I get to work at about 8.30 and spend an hour dealing with my mail. From 9.30 to 12.00, I telephone our suppliers. I usually have lunch in the canteen between 12.30 and 2.00. We have a general meeting from 2.00 to 3.00, and then, from 3.00 until about 5.00, I look at samples and discuss possible new suppliers. I leave at about 5.30 and get home at about 7.00. It's a long day, but I love the job.

Before I became a buyer, I was a fashion designer. I enjoyed designing, but I wanted a change. At home, I like to paint and listen to music. It helps me to relax. In the future, I would like to run my own clothes business. Or perhaps I can be a supplier for Marks & Spencer!

2 It is a normal day. What's Linda doing at these times?

a 1 p.m. *She's having lunch.*
b 7.45 a.m.
c 9 a.m.
d 4 p.m.
e 11 p.m.

3 Look at these two sentences. Why are the tenses different?

Linda has lunch between 12.30 and 2.00.
It's one o'clock, so Linda is having lunch.

LANGUAGE NOTE

The Present Continuous

We use the Present Continuous tense to talk about:

1 present projects *I'm learning English.*
2 actions happening now, at this moment *I'm reading this sentence.*
3 temporary situations *I'm working from home this week.*

It is different from the Present Simple tense (see page 9), which we use to talk about:

1 regular/habitual actions *I have lunch between one o'clock and two o'clock.*
2 permanent/fixed situations *I work for Marks & Spencer.*

We form the Present Continuous tense with the verb *to be* and the main verb with an *-ing* ending.

She works. (Present Simple) *She is working.* (Present Continuous)

When speaking, we normally use contracted forms of the verb *to be.*

I'm	*he's*	*we're*	
you're	*she's*	*they're*	*working.*
	it's		

Present Continuous
Linda is working on a new project.
I'm calling you about your order.
She is wearing a suit.
She's having lunch in a restaurant today.

Present Simple
Linda works for Marks & Spencer.
I call every client four times a month.
She often wears jewellery.
Usually she has a quick lunch.

B

LANGUAGE FOCUS

Look at these sentences. They are all in the Present Simple form. Make another sentence using the same verb in the Present Continuous. The first one is done for you.

1	I **call** my suppliers every day.	*I can't talk long, **I'm calling** from Paris.*
2	I **read** every day on the train.	At the moment, I ...
3	I **smoke** twenty cigarettes a day.	I've got a cold so ...
4	It **rains** a lot here.	Oh, no! It ...
5	We usually **stay** at the Hotel Bristol.	This time, ...
6	She **wears** very smart suits.	Today, ...
7	Most days she **writes** reports.	This morning, she....

C

LISTENING AND QUESTION-MAKING

Linda's colleague Michael calls her from Australia. It is 10.30 a.m.

1 Listen to the conversation and fill in the spaces.

A: Linda Dawson.
B: Hi, Linda. It's Michael.
A: Michael! How's it going? Where are you?
B: I'm in .... I'm .... from the hotel.
A: .... in Sydney?
B: It's half past eight, in the evening. Actually, ... right now. I'm calling from the restaurant.
A: Is it urgent, Michael? I'm rather busy.
B: No. Just a few questions. It can wait.
A: Sorry, Michael. .... for the sales meeting. What are you having?
B: Having?
A: For dinner. What are you .... ?
B: Oh! Lobster.
A: Enjoy your lobster. .... in a couple of hours?
B: Sure. That's fine.
A: Great. Bye.
B: Bye.

2 Make questions for these answers. The first one is done for you.

a	*What is Linda doing?*	She's checking the sales figures.
b		He's calling from Sydney.
c		At a hotel.
d		He's having dinner.
e		Lobster.

D

VOCABULARY

Look again at the text in C. Find the expressions which mean the same as the ones below. The first one is done for you.

1 In fact *Actually*
2 I have a lot of things to do
3 How are things?
4 I'm preparing for
5 We can talk about it later
6 In two hours' time

E

PRACTICE

Decide if the verbs in these sentences are in the correct form. If they are wrong, correct them.

1 ○ Where are you working this week?
● In our Brussels office.

2 ○ Cigarette?
● No, thanks. I'm not smoking.

3 I can't come now – I speak to a customer.

4 ○ Where are you staying?
● At the Holiday Inn.

5 Are you enjoy your stay?

6 How many weeks' holiday are you having every year?

7 We are launching a new product today.

8 ○ What do you do?
● I phone our head office.

F

LISTEN AND REPLY

Listen to what the person is saying and reply in a natural way.

G

SPEAKING

Imagine you are on a business trip abroad. Call you partner and tell them what you are doing.

5.2 Company developments

Countable and uncountable expressions

a few / a little *not much / not many*

SEE LANGUAGE FILES: 4, 12

A

SPEAKING

1 Which stores are famous in your country? What do they sell? Are they also famous abroad?

2 Which British or American stores do you know?

3 You are advising a British or American store that wants to open in your country. What changes do they need to make for the store to be a success?

B

READING

1 Read the article on the opposite page about Marks & Spencer.

2 Answer the following questions about the Marks & Spencer article.

a Where is the company building a new store?
b What does M&S sell?
c What is M&S studying at the moment?
d How many people does the company employ?
e What varies from country to country?
f What are more and more people doing?

3 Which questions in **2** above are in the Present Simple tense? Why? Which questions are in the Present Continuous tense? Why?

C

VOCABULARY

Look again at the article and find words to match these definitions.

1 sales income
2 an agreement to use a company's name in return for a fee
3 a company which sells items to another company
4 people who use a particular shop or firm
5 how long an item remains on sale

MARKS & SPENCER

A BRITISH SUCCESS STORY

Marks & Spencer, the British food and clothes company, is the most famous British shop in the world. At the moment, there are 283 M&S shops in Britain, and other shops in France, Belgium, Holland, Spain, and Portugal. Currently, they are building a large new store in Paris on the rue de Rivoli. In North America, the company owns Brooks Brothers and there are about fifty stores in Canada. More and more people, from Hong Kong to Lisbon, are buying their clothes and food from M&S.

The company employs about 50,000 people worldwide. Sales have increased by 80% over the last ten years, mainly due to expansion overseas. Many of the shops abroad are franchises. Owners of franchises buy all their stock from Marks & Spencer and pay the company a percentage of their turnover.

The clothes vary from country to country. In Thailand, for example, M&S sell more short-sleeved shirts because of the climate. In Japan, they sell smaller sizes because of the average size of the population. In Austria, they stock very large clothes. Food departments sell typically British food: tea, cake, biscuits, etc., and the shops in Paris are very popular at lunchtime for the sale of sandwiches.

Why is Marks & Spencer so successful? The standards of quality are very high. All suppliers have regular inspections. All customers can return any item which they think is unsatisfactory. Stocks are limited. Shelf lives are short. This means that items only stay in the shop for six to seven weeks. Eighty per cent of the suppliers are British; in fact, M&S buys twenty per cent of the total cloth produced in Britain. Prices are high, but so is the quality. In Britain, one man in five buys his suits at M&S, and one woman in three buys her underwear there.

What about the future? At the moment, the company is studying plans for development in Eastern Europe, Japan, and even China. Next century, it is possible that one Chinese in five will wear Marks & Spencer suits. That's a lot of suits!

D QUESTION-MAKING AND VOCABULARY

A journalist is interviewing a director of Marks & Spencer about the success of his company.

1 Here are the director's answers. Write down the interviewer's questions. The first one is done for you.

a	*How many Marks & Spencer shops are there?*	There are 283 in Britain, and 150 overseas.
b		About 50,000 worldwide.
c		The one main reason for our success is quality. The suppliers give us high-quality products and we offer our customers a very good service.
d		Yes, there's a lot of competition between retailers. Clothes and food are products which everyone needs.
e		Yes. We are thinking about expanding into Eastern Europe and the Far East, particularly China.

2 Look at the director's answers in **1** above. Find the words he uses which mean the same as the words below, and write them in the table. The first one is done for you.

a especially
b abroad
c all over the world
d growing bigger
e companies which make products for other companies
f people who buy products
g companies which sell products to the public
h the thing a company sells

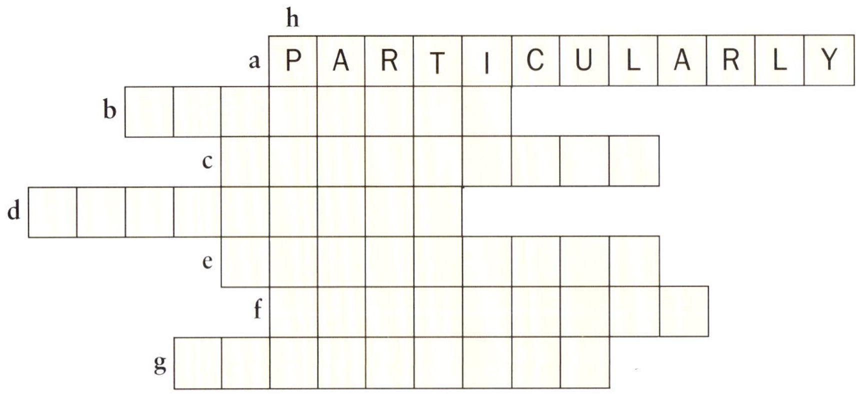

LANGUAGE NOTE

Countable and uncountable expressions

As we saw in Unit 3, some nouns are countable (C) and others are uncountable (U). Here are some more expressions we use to talk about countable and uncountable nouns.

In this business ***there is a lot of*** *competition.*
How many *stores* ***are there*** *in Britain?*
There are not many *towns in England without a Marks & Spencer store.*

	(C)	(U)
Singular	*There's a ...*	*There's (some)...*
Plural	*There are a lot of/many...* *a few...*	*There's a lot of...* *a little...*
Negative	*There aren't any...*	*There isn't much..* *(any)...*
Question	*Are there any... ?* *How many [...] are there?*	*Is there any... ?* *How much [...] is there?*

E

LANGUAGE FOCUS

1 Are these nouns countable or uncountable? Mark them C or U.

customer	figure	clothes
information	order	people
employee	money	competitor
company	person	competition

2 Choose an appropriate phrase from the Language Note above to complete the sentences. (Sometimes there is more than one possible answer.) The first one is done for you.

a There *aren't* *many* companies in the world with more than 100,000 employees.

b How .... employees .... in your company?

c ○ .... information about prices in your brochure?
● No, there .... We have a separate price list.

d ○ How .... money do you spend on advertising?
● Not .... We rely on word of mouth.

e ○ .... there .... competition from companies in the Far East?
● Yes, there .... , particularly from Japan.

5.3 Personal developments

Meeting someone you know

How are things? *How's business?*

SEE LANGUAGE FILE: 9

A

LISTENING

1 What do you say when you

a meet someone for the first time?
b see someone for the first time in five years?

2 Now listen to these two conversations between Jim Fenton and Bruno Retter, and say if the sentences below are true (T) or false (F).

Conversation One, 1990

Conversation Two, 1995

Conversation One	T	F
a Bruno and Jim know each other.	☐	☐
b Jim works for Global Systems.	☐	☐
c Bruno knows Jim's company.	☐	☐
d Bruno is a Sales Manager.	☐	☐
e Bruno doesn't know many people at the party.	☐	☐

Conversation Two	T	F
a Simons International isn't doing very well.	☐	☐
b The company is moving to new offices.	☐	☐
c Global Systems is having a good year.	☐	☐
d Bruno knows Jim's family.	☐	☐
e Jim is looking for a new job.	☐	☐

3 Now listen to Conversation Two again, and complete these sentences.

a Simons International .... to new offices.
b The company .... new staff.
c Things .... going very well at Global Systems.
d The company .... orders.
e Jim's wife .... at the hospital.
f His son .... for his exams.
g His daughter .... France.

4 a Can you remember any of the questions Bruno and Jim ask each other? Write them down.
b Now listen to Conversation Two. Check your answers.

LANGUAGE NOTE

Meeting someone you know

Meeting someone for the first time
How do you do?
Pleased to meet you.

Meeting someone you know
How's your wife/family?
How are things going?
How's business?
How's your daughter doing in her new job?

A number of responses to these '*How...*' questions are possible.

Very well.
Fine.
Not so bad.
Not very well, I'm afraid.

Responding to good news
That's good (news).
I'm pleased to hear that.

Responding to bad news
That's bad news.
I'm sorry to hear that.

B

PRACTICE

1 Choose possible responses to sentences a-g. Sometimes there is more than one correct answer. The first one is done for you.

a How's your family?
1 They're all well. ✓
2 They're very well. ✓
3 They're very fine. ✗

b How are you?
1 Not so bad.
2 It's not very well, I'm afraid.
3 Pleased to meet you.

c How's your new assistant doing?
1 He's going fine.
2 He's doing well.
3 Fine thanks, and you?

d How's business?
1 Not very well.
2 It's going well.
3 Yes, it is.

e Business is going very well.
1 That's good news.
2 I'm sorry to hear that.
3 I'm pleased to hear that.

f She isn't very well, I'm afraid.
1 I'm sorry to hear that.
2 That's good.
3 Too bad.

g How about you?
1 I'm fine, too.
2 I'm very well, too.
3 That's bad news.

2 Complete each space with one of these words. Use each word once only.

pleased	parents	doing	isn't
wife	sorry	job	going

1 How's your .... going?
2 How's your .... doing in her new job?
3 He's .... very well in his new company.
4 How are your .... ?
5 I'm .... to hear that things are .... well.
6 I'm .... to hear that your husband .... very well.

QUESTION-MAKING

Here are some answers. What are the questions? (For example, 1 = *How are you?*)

D

PAIR WORK

You meet your partner for the first time in three months. Find out what is happening in their life. Ask your partner about their company, job, English course, family, and answer your partner's questions.

Before you begin, **invent** some news to tell your partner about:

your job (good news, bad news)
your family (your wife or husband, your brother/sister)
other people (your boss/teacher, your colleague, your new assistant)

6

Arrangements

6.1 Future engagements

Present continuous for future

I'm flying on... *When are you leaving?*

SEE LANGUAGE FILES: 3, 12

A LISTENING

Diana Anderson and Tom Carter work for the same company. Diana is Sales Director and Tom is Marketing Director. They are talking about their appointments for next week.

1 Some of the information in Diana's and Tom's diaries is not correct. Listen to Part One, and make the necessary changes to their diaries.

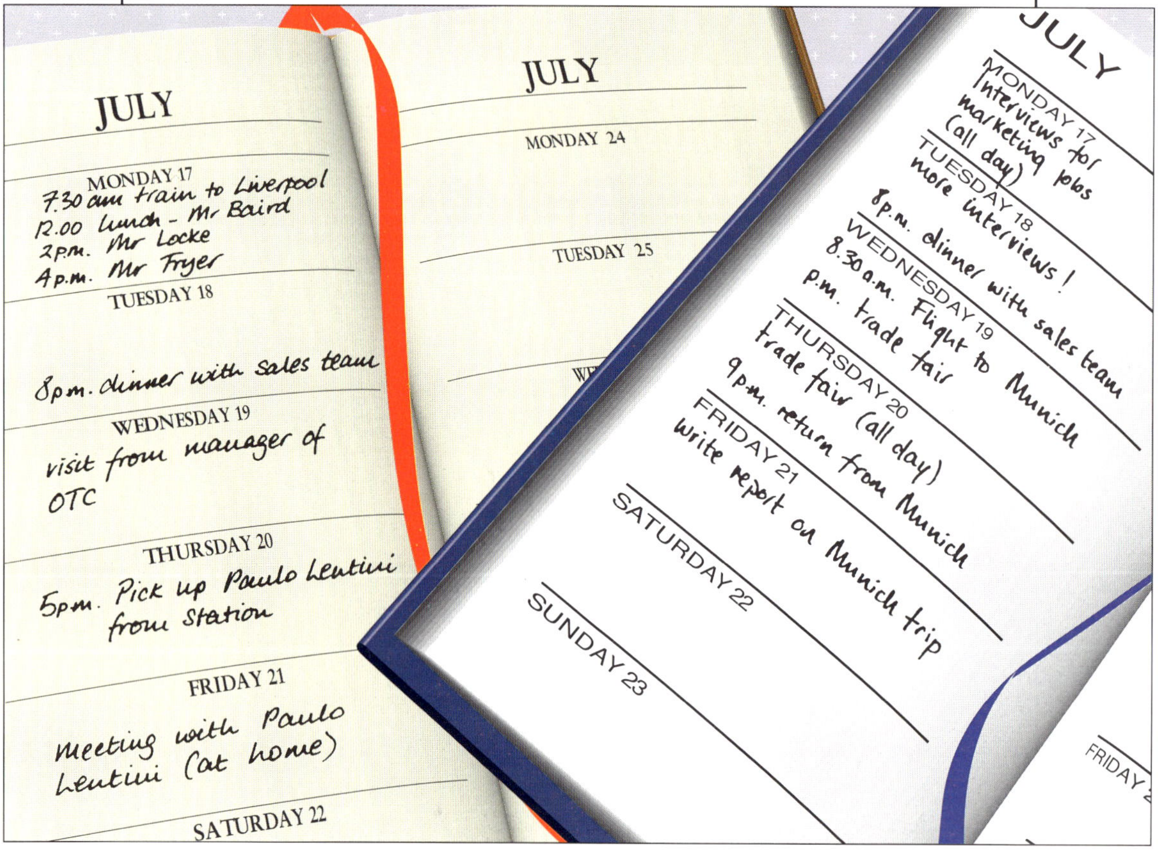

2 In Part Two of the dialogue, Diana talks about her plans for next week. Before you listen, try and complete the spaces in the text below.

T What .... next week, Diana?
D .... the train to Liverpool on Monday morning, and I'm .... three clients in the afternoon. Then, on Wednesday, the Manager of OTC .... – I'm .... him round the company. Oh, before I forget, ... dinner with the sales team on Tuesday evening -– I hope you're free.
T Yes, I am. .... candidates for the marketing job all day Monday and Tuesday, but .... in the evening.
D OK, good.

3 Now listen to Part Two and check your answers.

LANGUAGE NOTE

The Present Continuous

In Unit 5 (page 63) we studied the Present Continuous tense for describing actions taking place at the moment of speaking.

I'm not working today.
Prices are rising.
The phone's ringing – please answer it.

We also use the Present Continuous to describe fixed plans and appointments in the future.

I'm flying to Munich on Wednesday.
They are having dinner with the sales team next week.
What are you doing at the weekend?

B PRACTICE AND PAIR WORK

Now look again at Diana's and Tom's appointments for next week.

1 Talk about them, using the Present Continuous.

On Monday, Diana is taking the train to Liverpool.

2 Work with a partner. Make some true and false sentences. Your partner must say if they are true or false.

You: *Tom is leaving for Munich on Monday.*
Your partner: *False. He's leaving on Wednesday.*

(Note that we stress the word *Wednesday* to show the correct answer: *Wednesday*, not *Monday*.)

C QUESTION-MAKING

Use words from the box to find questions for the answers in 1-5. Take one word or phrase from each column. The first one is done for you.

Where		*Diana*	*working in his office*	*on Thursday?*
Why	*is*	*Tom*	*visiting*	*on Wednesday?*
What	*are*	*Diana and Tom*	*doing*	*on Tuesday evening?*
When	*isn't*	*the Manager of OTC*	*travelling*	*Diana?*
How			*flying*	*to Liverpool?*

1 *What are Diana and Tom doing on Tuesday evening?*
They are having dinner with the sales team.
2 .... ? By train.
3 .... ? To Munich.
4 .... ? On Wednesday.
5 .... ? Because he's still at the trade fair.

D PRACTICE

Find out what your partner is doing later today, later this week, this weekend, and next week. Have conversations like this:

	next week/next Monday, etc.?
What are you doing...	*tomorrow /the day after tomorrow?*
Where are you going...	*this evening/this week/this Friday, etc.?*
	on Saturday/Sunday, etc.?

I'm working all day. What about you?
I'm staying at home. I'm re-decorating my house.

E READING

Mr Keller works in the travel business. He has a very busy week. Read the information and complete the page from his diary on page 77.

1 Tomorrow, he's flying to New York.
2 The day after tomorrow, he has two afternoon appointments.
3 On Saturday, he attended a trade fair in Prague.
4 Today, he's seeing the Managing Director of Ocean Travel.
5 He's returning from New York in three days' time.
6 He returned from Prague yesterday.
7 He's spending this weekend at his holiday home in Kiel.
8 In New York, he's meeting Mrs Catell at 3 p.m., and Mrs Forster two hours later.
9 The day before yesterday, he went sightseeing in Prague.
10 Next Monday, his contact from Transcape is coming to visit him.

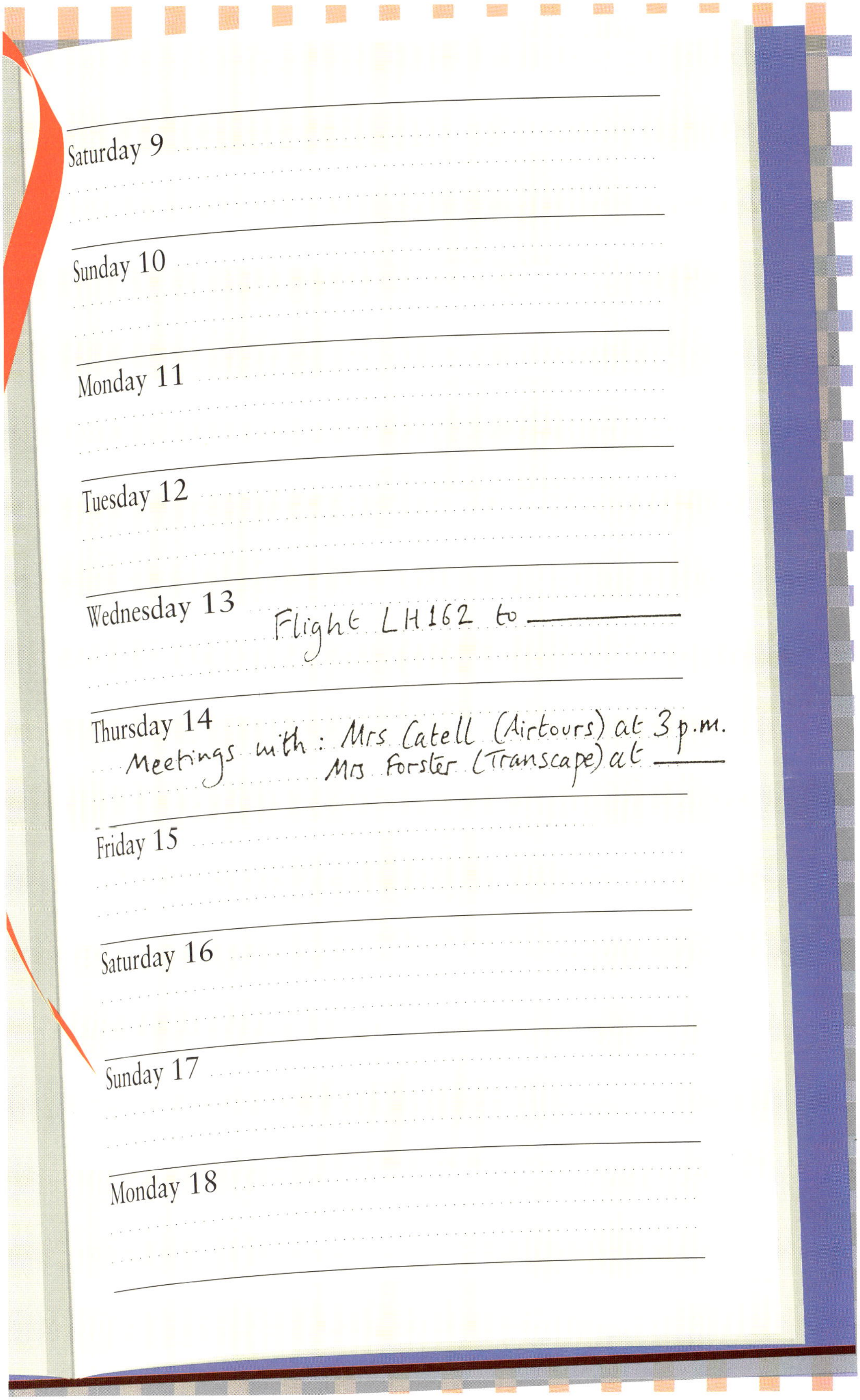
Saturday 9
Sunday 10
Monday 11
Tuesday 12
Wednesday 13
Flight LH162 to
Thursday 14
Meetings with: Mrs Catell (Airtours) at 3 p.m.
Mrs Forster (Transcape) at
Friday 15
Saturday 16
Sunday 17
Monday 18

6.2 Fixing the date

Ordinal numbers
first second third

SEE LANGUAGE FILES: 1, 3, 12

San Francisco Earthquake

First man on moon

A SPEAKING

How important are dates in your working life?

1 a What dates are public holidays in your country?

b Do you think your country has too many public holidays or not enough?

2 Do you celebrate birthdays at work? Do you think it is a good idea?

3 Do you keep a diary? How far ahead do you plan your appointments? (one month? six months? a year? longer?)

Unification of East and West Germany

Assassination of President Kennedy

B LISTENING

1 The pictures show some famous historical events. Can you name the year and month when they happened?

2 Now listen and match the date you hear with the correct picture.

PRACTICE

1 Say the months of the year. (Mark the stressed syllables).

January	April	July	October
February	May	August	November
March	June	September	December

Now listen and check your answers.

2 Which are your favourite and least favourite months? Why?

3 Write the next two numbers in each sequence. The first one is done for you.

a 1st, 2nd, 3rd, 4th, *5th*, *6th*
b 7th, 9th, 11th, 13th, ... , ... ,
c 19th, 20th, 21st ..... , ... ,
d 29th May, 30th May, ... , ... ,
e June 16, June 17, June 18, ... , ... ,
f 1.4.95, 1.5.95, 1.6.95, ... , ... , *

4 Now say the numbers aloud.

5 The Date Game

Write down these dates (in numbers, not in words).

A your birthday	**B** today's date	**C** tomorrow's date
D yesterday's date	**E** the day after Wednesday the thirtieth of May	**F** the date of Christmas Day last year
G the date of your last holiday	**H** the date of the last day of this century	**I** the date you started working for your company
J the date of your country's main public holiday	**K** the date you started learning English	**L** the most memorable date in your life!

6 Now read the dates to your partner in a different order. Your partner listens, and then matches each date with the description above.

You: *The thirty-first of December, nineteen ninety-nine*
Your partner: *The last day of this century*

* See the Language Note on page 80.

LANGUAGE NOTE

Dates

We use ordinal numbers (see Language File 1, page 163) for dates.
the first of March
the twenty-ninth of September

There is a difference between the British and American way of saying dates. This is important when we write dates using figures only.

In British English, we say the day first, then the month, then the year.
1.4.95 = *the first of April, nineteen ninety-five*
8.6.95 = *the eighth of June, nineteen ninety-five*

In American English, we say the month first, then the day, then the year.
1.4.95 = *January fourth, nineteen ninety-five*
8.6.95 = *August sixth, nineteen ninety-five*

D

PAIR WORK

You and your partner are organizing an international conference in London. You are meeting the representatives when they arrive, so you need their arrival dates, times, and destinations.

Person A: Turn to File J, page 159.
Person B: Prepare the questions you need to ask to complete your table. Then ask your partner the questions.

What date is Mr Gardini arriving?

Name	Nationality	Arriving at:	Date	Time
Mr Sato	Japanese	Manchester Airport	10 June	22.10
Mr Mason	American	Heathrow Airport	11 June	14.30
Mr Jacobsen		Victoria Station		13.27
Mrs Moinard	French	Victoria Station	12 June	11.12
Mr Gardini		Heathrow Airport		16.15
	German	Gatwick Airport		
Mrs Lacunza	Spanish			05.45

E

LISTENING

Two of the conference organizers are arranging to meet the representatives at their point of arrival, but they don't have the correct information.

Listen to the six dialogues and the information in the completed table in D. Which three people will have nobody to meet them?

6.3 Getting connected

Telephone language
Who's calling? This is...

SEE LANGUAGE FILE: 8

A

VOCABULARY

The language we use on the telephone is not always the same as when we are face to face with a person.

1 Write the telephone expressions which mean the same as the expressions on the left. (The first one is done for you.)

	Face to face	On the telephone
a	What's your name?	Could I have your name, please?
b	I'm John Davis.	T....... .... John Davis.
c	● Are you Mrs Dimbleby?	I .... Mrs Dimbleby?
	○ Yes, I am.	S ....
d	Could you wait a moment?	H....... the l......., please.

2 Are there special telephone expressions in your language? Does everyone use them?

B

LISTENING

Mr Pym of Technos wants to speak to Mr Jones from Lakefield's. He has three conversations with the switchboard operator.

1 Listen to the three conversations. After each conversation, answer these questions.

a Does Mr Pym speak to Mr Jones? If not, why not?
b Does Mr Pym leave a message? What does he say?

2 Can you remember any of the telephone expressions you heard in the three conversations?

C

LISTENING AND SPEAKING

The flowchart opposite shows Mr Pym's three conversations. Each path represents a different conversation.

The path on the **left** shows Conversation One.
The path on the **right** shows Conversation Two.
The path in the **middle** shows Conversation Three.

1 Listen to the three conversations again, and fill in the spaces (1-9) in the flowchart.

2 Practise the different conversations with a partner.

D

PAIR WORK

You and your partner are going to have four telephone conversations (A-D). Use the flowchart opposite to help you prepare what you are going to say.

CONVERSATION A:
Person A: You want to speak to Mr Harmer in the Personnel Department of Lakefield's. Call Lakefield's. Don't leave a message. Say you'll call back later.
Person B: You are the switchboard operator at Lakefield's. Mr Harmer's line is engaged. Ask the caller if he or she wants to hold on.

CONVERSATION B:
Person A: You are the switchboard operator at Lakefield's. Mrs Walters is having lunch. Take a message if necessary.
Person B: You want to speak to Mrs Walters in the Sales Department of Lakefield's. Leave her a message to say you will call again at 2 p.m.

CONVERSATION C:
Person A: You want to speak to Mr Harmer in the Personnel Department of Lakefield's. If he's not there, leave a message to ask him to call you back.
Person B: You are the switchboard operator at Lakefield's. Mr Harmer is on another line. Ask the caller if he wants to hold on.

CONVERSATION D:
Person A: You are Mr Harmer. Call back Person A to see what he or she wants.
Person B: Mr Harmer calls you. Tell him his car is parked in front of your garage. Can he move it, please?

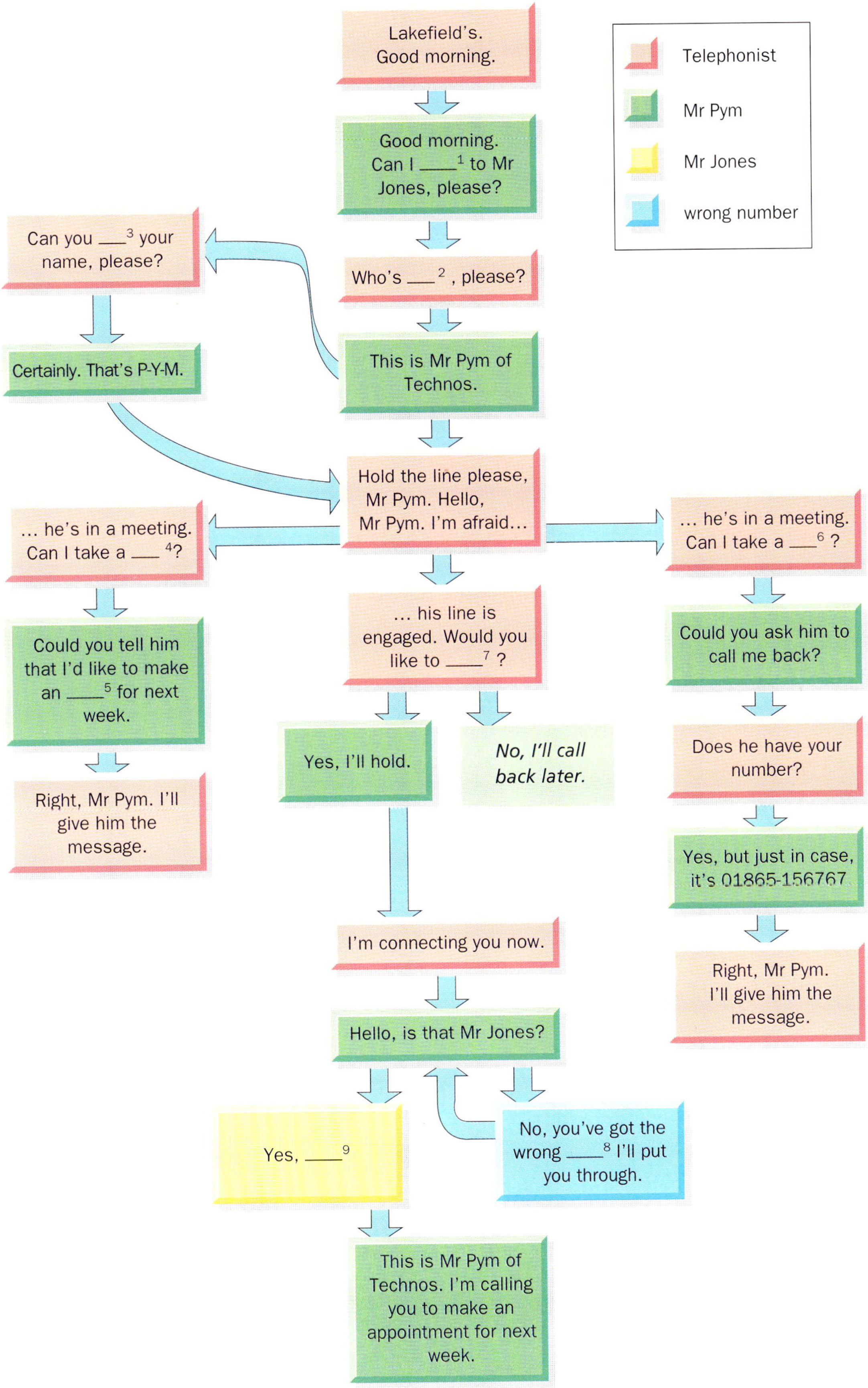
Telephonist
Mr Pym
Mr Jones
wrong number
Lakefield's. Good morning.
Good morning. Can I ____1 to Mr Jones, please?
Who's ____2, please?
This is Mr Pym of Technos.
Can you ____3 your name, please?
Certainly. That's P-Y-M.
Hold the line please, Mr Pym. Hello, Mr Pym. I'm afraid…
… he's in a meeting. Can I take a ____4?
Could you tell him that I'd like to make an ____5 for next week.
Right, Mr Pym. I'll give him the message.
… his line is engaged. Would you like to ____7 ?
Yes, I'll hold.
No, I'll call back later.
… he's in a meeting. Can I take a ____6 ?
Could you ask him to call me back?
Does he have your number?
Yes, but just in case, it's 01865-156767
Right, Mr Pym. I'll give him the message.
I'm connecting you now.
Hello, is that Mr Jones?
Yes, ____9
No, you've got the wrong ____8 I'll put you through.
This is Mr Pym of Technos. I'm calling you to make an appointment for next week.

E

PRONUNCIATION

In rapid speech, a word beginning with a vowel (a, e, i, o, u) is usually linked in pronunciation with the end of the preceding word.

He's not‿in the office‿at the moment.

1 Listen to these sentences and repeat them.

I'm‿afraid his line's‿engaged.

I'm‿afraid he's‿in‿a meeting‿at the moment.

2 Mark the linked words in these sentences.

Could I leave a message?

Could you ask Alan to call me back?

I'm afraid he's on another line.

I don't know if he's at home or not.

I'll pass on the message as soon as I see him.

3 Now listen to check your answers and repeat what you hear.

F

PRACTICE

Sentences **a-e** all have mistakes. Can you correct them?

a I'm afraid but he's not here.

....

b I call you about the contract.

....

c Can I to take a message?

....

d Can you tell him to me call back?

....

e I call back later.

....

6.4 Appointments

Making and changing appointments

How about... ? *That suits me.*

PRACTICE

1 Lisa Yates wants to make an appointment to see Martin Lennon. Complete Martin's half of the dialogue with sentences a to h.

Lisa	Hello, is that Martin?
Martin	.... (1)
Lisa	Hello, Martin. This is Lisa.
Martin	.... (2)
Lisa	I'd like to make an appointment to see you next week.
Martin	.... (3)
Lisa	How about Wednesday?
Martin	.... (4)
Lisa	No, I'm afraid **I'm** busy that day.
Martin	.... (5)
Lisa	Yes, that's fine. What suits you better – morning or afternoon?
Martin	.... (6)
Lisa	How about 2.30?
Martin	.... (7)
Lisa	OK. See you next Friday at half past two, then.
Martin	.... (8)

Martin's words:

a What about Friday?
b After lunch is more convenient.
c Of course. What day suits you?
d Yes, speaking.
e Yes, that's fine.
f No, I'm afraid I'm attending a sales conference. Is Thursday convenient?
g Hi, Lisa. What can I do for you?
h Great. I look forward to it.

2 Do you think that Martin and Lisa:

a don't know each other?
b are working together for the first time?
c know each other well?

Choose just one answer.

B

LANGUAGE FOCUS

Complete sentences **a** and **b** so they mean the same as the sentence *in italics*. Use expressions from the dialogue in A to help you.

1 *What day do you prefer?*
  a What day .... you?
  b What day is .... for you?

2 *How about Wednesday?*
  a .... Wednesday convenient?
  b .... Wednesday suit you?

3 *Sunday's convenient for me.*
  a Sunday .... me.
  b Sunday .... fine for me.

4 *I can't make it on Friday.*
  a Friday .... convenient for me.
  b Friday .... suit me.

C

PAIR WORK

Have a conversation to practise making an appointment, following these notes.

Person A: Mr/Ms Simpson | **Person B: Mr/Ms Yarnton**

A: Ask to speak to Mr/Ms Yarnton.

B: You are Mr/Ms Yarnton. *Speaking.*

A: Say hello. Explain that you want to make an appointment for next week.

B: Agree. Ask if 25th is convenient.

A: No, you're in the USA. Ask if 26th is OK.

B: No, you're at a conference. Suggest 27th.

A: Agree. Ask if he/she prefers the morning or the afternoon.

B: Afternoon. Ask what time suits him/her.

A: Suggest 4.30 p.m.

B: Confirm the arrangement.

LANGUAGE NOTE

Changing appointments

We can change an appointment in one of three ways.

We can **bring it forward** to an earlier date.

Or, we can **postpone** it to a later date.

Or, we can **cancel** it completely.

D LISTENING

Three people telephone Lawson and Fowles to change their appointments. They either bring forward, postpone, or cancel their appointments.

Listen, and change the secretary's appointments diary for Wednesday and Thursday.

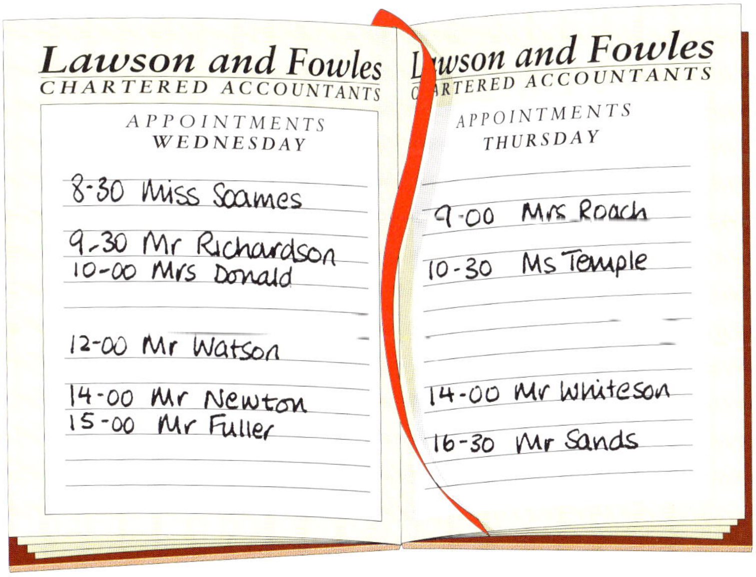

E PAIR WORK

Person A: You are one of the people on the list in D. Call to postpone, bring forward, or cancel your appointment.

Person B: You are the secretary. Make the necessary change(s) to the appointments diary in D.

7

Describing and comparing

7.1 Comparing

Comparative and superlative adjectives

faster   *more comfortable*   *the best*

SEE LANGUAGE FILE: 6

A

VOCABULARY AND SPEAKING

1 The adjectives in the right-hand column are the opposites of the ones on the left (a-e). Write in the missing letters and match them up. The first one is done for you.

a	comfortable	*slow*
b	fast	c _ _ _ _
c	dangerous	i _ _ _ _ _ _ _ _ _ _
d	expensive	u _ _ _ _ _ _ _ _ _ _ _ _
e	efficient	s _ _ _

2 Discuss these questions in pairs or groups.

1 How often do you travel?
2 Do you prefer to travel by plane, by car, or by train?
3 What are the advantages of each? And what are the disadvantages? Compare them using the adjectives in **1**.

B

LISTENING

Robert Dillon is in England on business. He has a meeting in Paris tomorrow evening. He must decide how to travel from London to Paris: by plane or by train. He is talking to a colleague.

1 Listen to the conversation and tick (✓) the correct box.

	Plane	Train
faster	☐	☐
cheaper	☐	☐
more comfortable	☐	☐
better	☐	☐

2 Here are some sentences from the Listening. Put the words in the right order. Then listen again and check your answers.

1 faster the is plane
2 train cheaper a little the is
3 day depends but the it time on of
4 comfortable definitely it more is

LANGUAGE NOTE

Adjectives for comparing

Adjective category	Example	Comparative	Superlative
one syllable	*quick*	*quicker*	*the quickest*
two syllables ending *-y*	*easy*	*easier*	*the easiest*
two or more syllables (not ending *-y*)	*convenient*	*more convenient*	*the most convenient*
	comfortable	*less comfortable*	*the least comfortable*
irregular forms	*good*	*better*	*the best*
	bad	*worse*	*the worst*
	far	*further*	*the furthest*

PRACTICE

Look at these tables and answer the questions.

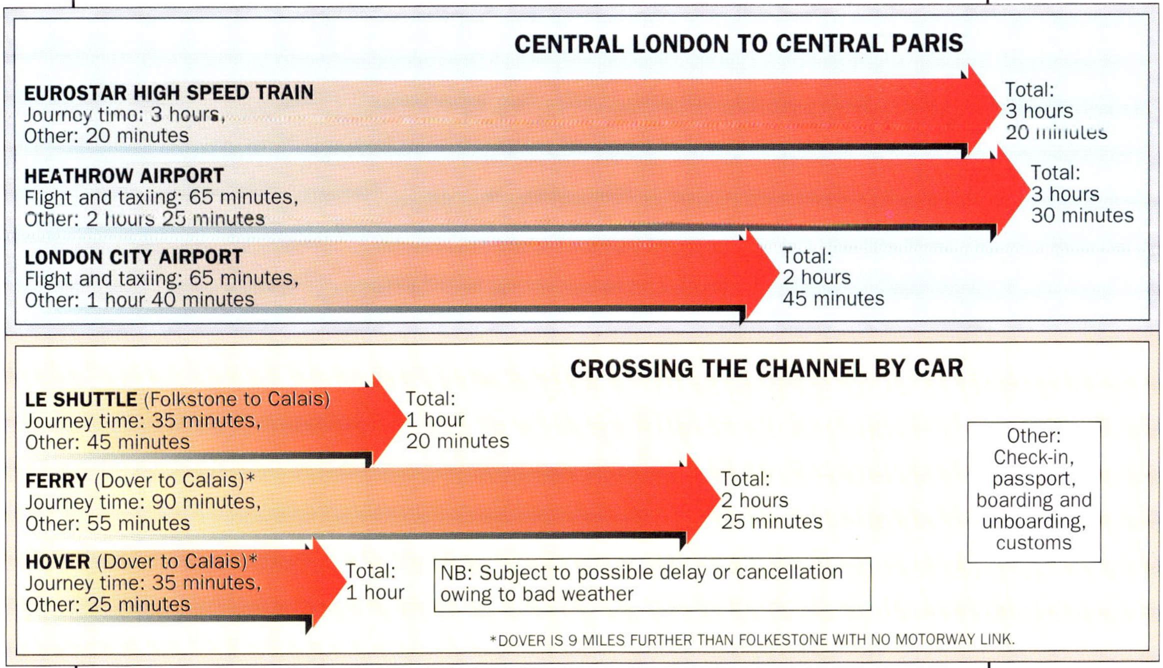

source: *Daily Telegraph*, 6 May 1994. All times given subject to change

1 What is the fastest way of crossing the Channel with a car?
2 What is the slowest way of crossing the Channel?
3 What is the safest way of crossing the Channel? Why?
4 What do you think is the best way of getting to Paris? Why?

D

READING

Channel Tunnel Quiz

1 Here are some questions about the Channel Tunnel between Great Britain and France. Can you guess the answers? (Each of the answers is one of the numbers in the list below).

50	15,000	220	10 bn	575	1,200	10	45

a What was the total cost of the project? *(... pounds)*
b How many workers died during the project?
c How deep is the tunnel below the sea-bed? *(... metres)*
d How many companies supplied equipment?
e How long is the total amount of railway track in the tunnel? *(... kilometres)*
f How long is the tunnel? *(... kilometres)*
g How heavy were the drilling machines? *(...tons)*
h How many workers built it?

2 Now read this article from the *Engineering Times* and check your answers.

"THE GREATEST ENGINEERING PROJECT EVER"

The Channel Tunnel is not just one tunnel; it consists of three tunnels, each thirty miles (about 50 km) long. It is the second longest tunnel in the world. The longest is the Seikan tunnel in Japan, but the Channel Tunnel has a longer under-sea section. Fifteen thousand workers built it (ten died in accidents) and 1,200 companies supplied equipment. It cost ten billion pounds to build.

One team began drilling in France and the other in England. The biggest problem for the builders was ensuring that the tunnels met at exactly the same place under the sea in the middle of the Channel. The drilling machines were the heaviest ever made, each weighing up to 575 tons. In the opinion of Roger Dobson, Director General of the Institute of Civil Engineers, 'The Channel Tunnel is the greatest engineering project ever.'

The tunnel itself is an average of 45 m below the sea-bed and has 220 km of railway track. It has the most sophisticated railway control system in the world, and will be the busiest railway track in Europe, with one train every three minutes.

E

PRONUNCIATION

1 Listen to these sentences. The words *in italics* are not stressed. How are they pronounced?

1 Swiss watches *are* more reliable *than* other watches.
2 Interest rates *are* lower in Britain *than* in France.
3 Champagne isn't *as* expensive *as* it was in the 1980s.
4 British Airways is more profitable *than* Air France.
5 This year there *are as* many tourists *as* last year.
6 The dollar is stronger *than* the pound.

2 Now listen again and repeat the sentences.

F

PRACTICE

1 Write sentences to compare the items in List A and List B. The first one is done for you.

List A	List B
The Channel Tunnel	The Seikan Tunnel

The Seikan Tunnel is longer than the Channel Tunnel.
The Channel Tunnel isn't as long as the Seikan Tunnel.

Canada	Luxembourg
A five-star hotel	A guest house
Mexican food	English food
The yen	The peseta
Antique furniture	Modern furniture
Learning English	Learning to drive
Tokyo	Rio de Janeiro
McDonalds	Burger King
Flying	Driving
Swiss watches	Taiwanese watches
Germans	Italians

2 Now make some more comparisons of your own.

7.2 Describing products

Describing physical qualities
It's round. It's made of...

A

VOCABULARY

1 Make lists of items which these adjectives can describe.

long	*pencil, corridor, train, book, ...*
thin	*credit card, ...*
rectangular	*TV screen, ...*
round	*compact disc, ...*
square	*computer disk, ...*

2 Make lists of products made of these materials.

glass	*window, ...*
plastic	*credit card, ...*
leather	*wallet, ...*
cardboard	*file, ...*
metal	*filing cabinet, ...*
wood	*table, ...*

LANGUAGE NOTE
Asking about products

What is it?	*It's a fax machine.*
What's it like?	*It's very small.*
What shape is it?	*It's rectangular.*
How large/big is it?	*It's 40 cm long by 30 cm wide.*
What colour is it?	*It's grey.*
What's it made of?	*It's made of plastic.*
Who's it made by?	*It's made by Canon.*
What's it for?	*It's for sending documents electronically.*
How much is it? *How much does it cost?*	*£375*

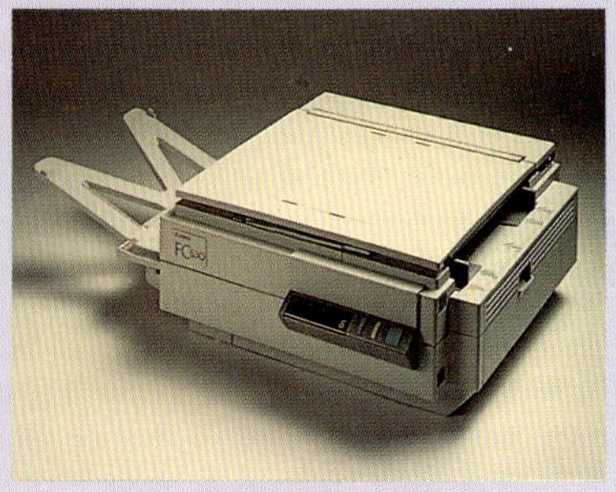

B

LISTENING AND SPEAKING

What's the product?

1 You are going to hear descriptions of four of the best inventions of the 1980s and 1990s. After each part of the description, you will hear a tone. When you hear the tone, stop the tape and try to guess which invention is being described. Then, continue listening and see if you were right. The person who guesses the product first wins.

1
2
3
4

2 Make a list of products. Your partner must guess the products in your list by asking you questions. Use the questions in the Language Note to help.

C

READING

Read these advertising slogans. What products are they for?

1 **The finest lager in the world.**

2 Cheapest London to New York

3 *It could not be clearer. Fresh from the springs of Scotland.*

4 Best picture – best colour

5 **The lightest portable on the market. Give your friends a call.**

6 **New version with larger memory and full colour screen**

7 ***Faster than Carl Lewis. More economical than a Rolls-Royce.***

D WRITING

Write slogans for some of these products and services.

1 a bank — *Lower interest rates from 1st January*
2 a supermarket
3 a language school
4 a dictionary
5 a fax machine
6 a new soft drink
7 an electric car
8 a travel agency
9 a printer
10 a video phone

E SPEAKING

Superlatives Quiz

1 Answer these questions. (The answers are in File M, page 160.)

a What is the largest company in the world?
☐ *AT&T* ☐ *Exxon* ☐ *IBM* ☐ *General Motors*

b Which is the richest country in the world?
☐ *Russia* ☐ *USA* ☐ *Germany* ☐ *UK*

c Where is the tallest building in the world?
☐ *Japan* ☐ *Canada* ☐ *USA* ☐ *China*

d Which country has the largest population?
☐ *Ireland* ☐ *China* ☐ *USA* ☐ *India*

e What is the longest river in the world?
☐ *Thames* ☐ *Seine* ☐ *Amazon* ☐ *Nile*

f Where is the fastest train in the world?
☐ *France* ☐ *Italy* ☐ *Spain* ☐ *Japan*

g Where is the longest bridge in the world?
☐ *Australia* ☐ *USA* ☐ *Peru* ☐ *Japan*

h Who was the youngest President of the USA?
☐ *Kennedy* ☐ *Roosevelt* ☐ *Carter* ☐ *Clinton*

2 Now write three or four more questions like these. Ask your partner or other members of the class.

7.3 Evaluating products

Asking for and giving opinions

What do you think? I agree. I feel...

A SPEAKING

1 What products are famous all over the world?
2 What countries do they come from?
3 Why are they so well-known?

B LISTENING

The guests on a radio programme are discussing the most successful products of the twentieth century.

1 Listen to the discussion and make a list of the products they mention.

2 Complete the spaces with the superlative form of the adjective in brackets. The first one is done for you.

a It's one of the (successful) *most successful* products.
b It's the (well-known) .... product of the century.
c It is the (stylish) .... product.
d It's one of the (cheap) .... and (practical) .... products of the century.
e They are the (popular) .... products with children.

3 Can you remember which products are being described in sentences a-e above? Listen again to check.

LANGUAGE NOTE

Asking opinions	Giving opinions	Agreeing/Disagreeing	
What do you think about... ?	*I feel...*	*I agree.*	*I disagree.*
How do you feel about... ?	*I think...*	*Definitely.*	
	In my opinion...	*Sure.*	

C

LANGUAGE FOCUS

Listen to the conversation in B again. Look at the list of expressions in the Language Note and tick (✓) the ones you hear.

D

PRACTICE

Have conversations with a partner. Here is an example dialogue for 1.

1 The best month to take a holiday (July? August? September?)

A
Ask B his/her opinion.
What do you think is the best month to take a holiday?

B
Give opinion + reason.
In my opinion, September is the best, because there aren't so many tourists.

B
Ask A his/her opinion.
Do you agree?/ What do you think?

A
Agree
Yes, I think so too.
or
Disagree. Give your opinion.
No, I disagree. I feel that July is the best because the weather is hotter.

2 The best food (French? Italian? Spanish? other?)
3 The best way to travel on business (by car? plane? train?)
4 The worst problem in the world today (pollution? unemployment? poverty?)
5 The most effective form of advertising (TV? newspapers? word of mouth?)
6 The most important invention of the twentieth century (the nuclear missile? the fax machine? the computer?)

E

SPEAKING

1 When do you think these products first appeared on the market?

1 Walkman

2 Scotch transparent tape

3 Tabasco sauce

4 Apple Macintosh computer

5 Ray Ban sunglasses

6 Monopoly board game

7 Swatch watch

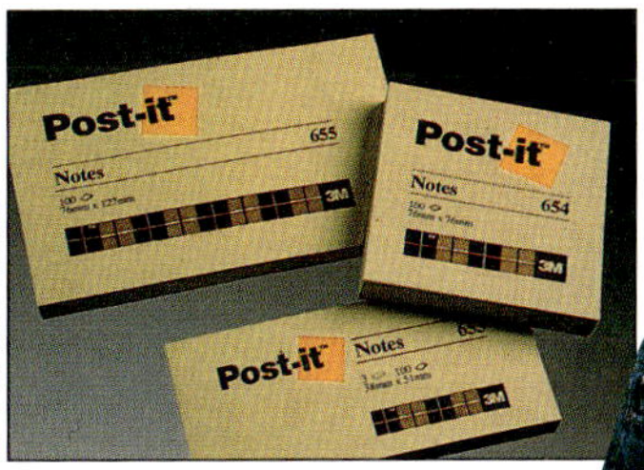

8 Post-It notes

9 Austin Mini motor car

10 Levis 501 jeans

11 Jumbo Jet aeroplane

12 Polaroid Camera

2 Work with a partner. Match the products above with the years below.

1930	1974	1890	1948	1959	1969
1983	1978	1935	1984	1868	1925

The answers are in File N, page 160.

8

Success stories

8.1 A life story

Past time references

In 1962… Two years ago…

SEE LANGUAGE FILES: 3, 14, 15

A

LISTENING AND SPEAKING

Sir Peter Parker is one of the best-known business people in Britain. He had many top management posts and was Chairman of British Rail for seven years.

1 Listen to the information about Sir Peter Parker's early life. What can you remember?

2 Listen again and answer the questions below.

a Where was he born?
b What did his parents do?
c How many brothers and sisters did he have?
d Why did the family leave China in 1937?
e Does he have any children?

3 Now listen again. Fill in the spaces.

19–	Born. .... August.
19–	Family moved to ....
1937	Family returned to England.
1939	Start of Second World War.
1942	Studied .... on special government-organized course.
19–	Joined army. Served as Intelligence Officer in .... , Burma, and ....
1947	.... army with rank of Major.
19–	Married Jill Rowe-Dutton.

READING

1 Read the article about Sir Peter Parker.

SIR PETER PARKER – A MAN OF MANY PARTS

Sir Peter Parker is well known as a top manager. He finally chose a career in business but there were always other things he wanted to do as well.

He studied history at Oxford University between 1947 and 1950, but he had many other interests. He wanted to be a sportsman: he played rugby for the University team and for his home town. He also wanted to be an actor and, when he was a student, he acted in a lot of plays. In 1948, he played the long and difficult role of Hamlet. He wanted to be a politician – in the same year, he was chairman of the University Labour Club. Three years later, he was a candidate for parliament in his home town, Bedford. He lost the election, but he increased his party's vote.

In 1956, Peter Parker organized a big international conference on 'The Human Problems of Industry'– the chairman was Prince Philip. He worked as a manager for a number of companies during the 1950s and 1960s, and later became well known to the public as Chairman of British Rail. He joined British Rail in 1976, and left in 1983. In 1978, he was awarded a knighthood by the Queen, and became Sir Peter Parker. He received another award from the Queen in 1993 for his 'contribution to public life'.

He is currently Chairman of several companies, including Mitsubishi Electric (UK), who appointed him in 1984. He was the first non-Japanese to become chairman of a Japanese company. In 1991, the Japanese Government awarded him the 'Grand Cordon of the Order of the Sacred Treasure.'

He wrote his autobiography, *For Starters*, in 1989.

2 For each photo, write the year and what happened in that year.

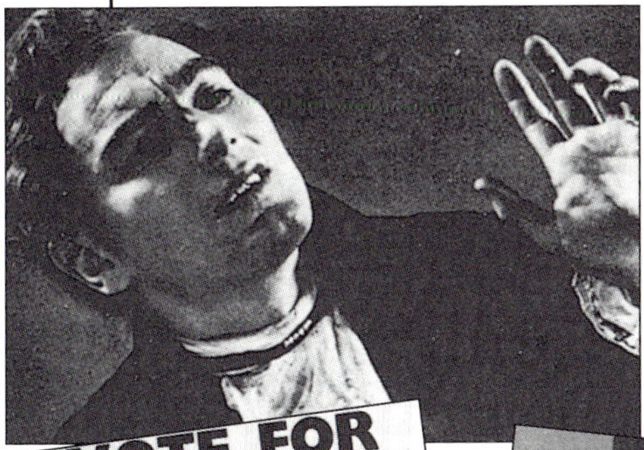

LANGUAGE NOTE

Past time references

1 We use these expressions to talk about a series of events in the past.

A year earlier ...
The following year ...
Three years later ...
Between 1947 and 1950 ...

2 We use *ago* to relate past events to now (the time of speaking or writing).

It's 1995. Sir Peter Parker was born sixty-nine years ago.

C

LANGUAGE FOCUS

With a partner, talk about the events of Sir Peter Parker's life. Look at the table in A and the article in B. Use the expressions in the Language Note.

D

PRACTICE

1 Write information about yourself in the table below.

	You	Your Partner
Place of birth:		
Place of education:		
Main subjects at school/university:		
Date of finishing education:		
First job:		
Starting date of first job:		
Date of joining present company:		
Date of starting present job:		

2 Now complete this text about yourself. Add extra details if you need to.

— I was born in ....
— I studied at ....
— My main subjects at school/university were ....
— I finished my studies .... ago, in ....
— .... later, I got my first job. I worked for .... as a ....
— I joined my present company .... ago, in ....
— I got my present job .... later, in ....

3 Read your text to your partner. Now listen to your partner's text and complete the right-hand column in the table.

8.2 Lending and borrowing

Financial vocabulary
save *afford* *owe*

A LANGUAGE FOCUS

Look at the cartoon and answer the questions that follow.

John: Can you lend me £1 for a sandwich?

Henry: Yes, of course. That will be £1.05 if you pay me back tomorrow, and £1.15 if you wait until Monday.

1 Who *can't afford* to buy a sandwich?
2 Who is *lending* the money?
3 Who is *borrowing* the money?
4 Who *owes* money to who?
5 Who will *spend* the money on a sandwich?
6 Who will pay *interest*?
7 Who will make a *profit*?
8 Who will make a *loss*?

B SPEAKING AND READING

1 Discuss the following, in pairs or groups.

a What is the best way to get rich in your country?
b How much money do you need to be rich?

2 Now read the article about Kenshin Oshima and answer the questions that follow.

KENSHIN OSHIMA MAKING MONEY OUT OF MONEY

For seven years, Kenshin Oshima had a very good job at the firm Mitsui and Co. But, at the age of 29, he did something very rare for a Japanese manager in his position — he resigned.

Oshima **earned** a good salary at Mitsui, but he wanted to make a lot of money, and to be very rich he needed to have his own company. He couldn't **afford** to start a company immediately, but during his years at Mitsui he spent very little money, and **saved** as much as he could.

In 1978, he **invested** his money, $236,500 in total, in his new company, Shohkoh Fund and Co. Shohkoh Fund specialized in **lending** money to businesses, but in small sums. This decision was a risk, as money-lending by private companies was not a respectable job in 1978. His first client was a firm in Tokyo, which **paid back** the money that it owed at an **interest** rate of 24%.

But his idea was good: his **profits** rose by 25% a year, and reached $38.5 million in 1992. He owns 80% of Shohkoh, and his shares in the company are now **worth** $997 million.

So, Oshima is now a billionaire, or nearly, but his strategy for the company is still the same: even now he specializes in smaller loans (a typical client **borrows** only $40,000), and he personally examines the references of every new client.

a When did Kenshin Oshima join Mitsui and Co.?
   1 At the age of 22.
   2 At the age of 29.
   3 In 1978.

b Why did he resign from his job?
   1 Because his salary was very high.
   2 Because he wanted to work for another company.
   3 Because he wanted to earn a lot of money.

c Why didn't he start his company before 1978?
   1 Because he spent a lot of money.
   2 Because he didn't want to be rich.
   3 Because he didn't have enough money.

d Where did he get the money to launch his business?
   1 He saved money from his salary.
   2 He borrowed it from a bank.
   3 A friend lent it to him.

e What does his company do?
   1 It owes money.
   2 It lends money.
   3 It borrows money.

C VOCABULARY

Look at the words **in bold** in the text in B. Fill in the spaces in these sentences with one of these words (in an appropriate form). Two are done for you.

A bank makes a *profit* (1) when it ....(2) money to its customers.

For example, a customer wants to buy a new car, but he can't ....(3) to pay for it, because he doesn't ....(4) enough money at work. So he goes to his bank manager and asks to ....(5) some money. But when he ....(6) the loan he also has to pay ....(7) on the money that he *owes* (8).

A bank is also a place where customers can make money. For example, they can ....(9) their money in a fixed interest account. With this type of account, they usually know what their money will be ....(10) in three or four years' time.

Alternatively, customers can ....(11) their capital in a portfolio of company ....(12) which is managed by the bank.

D LISTENING

A bank manager and his client are talking about a loan. The client, Mr Regan, wants to borrow some money to buy a flat.

1 Listen and complete these notes.

CENTRAL BANK PLC
Loan Application Form

Name:	*REGAN*	First name(s):	*JOHN PATRICK*
Price of house or flat:	£		
Personal savings:	£	Sum borrowed:	£
Monthly salary + other income:	£		
Repayment period:	years		
Monthly repayment:	£	Interest rate:	%

2 The bank manager says:
I think we may have a little problem here, Mr Regan.

What is the problem? What are the possible solutions?

E

SPEAKING

Discuss the following with a partner:

1 Do people usually buy or rent their houses or flats in your country?
2 Where do most people get the money to buy their houses?
3 When people borrow money for a house or flat, what is the usual repayment period? Are interest rates fixed or variable?

F

READING AND VOCABULARY

Match the headline (**1-4**) with the extract from the article (a-d).

a **BANK INTEREST RATES RISE**

b "SPEND, SPEND, SPEND" SAYS PRIME MINISTER

1 The last three months were no better for Sofimat, which made a loss of £150,000. The MD Alan Wilson said that he couldn't even afford to pay his staff in June.

3 "Now is not the time to save your money. There are too many companies out there waiting for you to buy their products. If you want to help industry, put your hand in your pocket."

c SHARE PRICE RISES TO HIGHEST LEVEL THIS YEAR

2 If you invested in EuroPac, your capital is now worth 35% more than this time last year. And the experts estimate that the price will continue to rise in the immediate future. So now is not the time to sell.

4 This is bad news for business, which faces another 0.5% increase in the cost of borrowing money. The last rise was only two months ago, when the rate went up by 1% to 8%.

d **SOFTWARE COMPANY REPORTS WORST FIGURES FOR 4 YEARS**

G

PRACTICE

With a partner, think of different ways of completing these sentences.

1 I spend my money on...
2 If I want to save my money, I can...
3 The best way to invest money is to...
4 I can afford (to)...
5 I can't afford (to)...
6 I owe money to...
7 A company makes a loss when...
8 I can borrow money from...

8.3 A family business

Sentence linkers

so but because

A PRONUNCIATION

Listen to these words. Are the vowel sounds underlined pronounced /ɜː/ or /ɔː/? Write them in the correct column. The first two are done for you.

learned	ordered	saw	bought
caught	returned	purchased	heard
imported	worked	earned	born
weren't	thought	launched	Sir

learned /ɜː/	caught /ɔː/

B READING AND SPEAKING

Gert Boyle

A Family Crisis

In 1970, Neal Boyle, Managing Director of Columbia Sportswear, borrowed a large sum of money from his bank to finance the business. As security for the loan, he offered his life insurance, his family house, and his wife's mother's house.

Three months later, he died. His wife Gert had no money, no job, and little work experience. She also had three children, including a son, Tim, who was at university.

Tim Boyle

What do you think Gert Boyle did next? What would you do in her situation?

C

PRACTICE

This is what happened to Columbia Sportswear after Neal Boyle's death.

1 Put the verbs in brackets into the correct past tense form. The first one is done for you.

1 Gert *decided* (decide) to run Columbia herself...
2 She .... (ask) the company accountant to resign...
3 Columbia .... (lose) many of their regular clients...
4 The bank manager .... (tell)Gert it was necessary to sell Columbia...
5 She .... (not/sell) the company...
6 Tim Boyle .... (join) the company straight from university at the age of 22. At university, he .... (study) journalism...
7 Gert and Tim .... (begin) to change the product range...
8 They .... (launch) a new product, the 'Bugaboo' jacket, in 1982...
9 Tim .... (become) President of Columbia...
10 The company .... (grow) during the 1980s...

2 Match the sentence-endings (a-j) below with 1-10 above. The first three are done for you.

a ...so they had very bad results. *3*
b ...because they had too many products that weren't profitable. *7*
c ...and in 1993, Columbia's turnover reached $193 million. *10*
d ...and it was a big success – they sold 1.5 million between 1982 and 1993.
e ...so he didn't have any business experience.
f ...but Gert didn't want to retire, so she decided to continue to work for the company.
g ...so she found someone who wanted to buy the company.
h ...because she needed money to repay her husband's loan.
i ...because the buyer offered her a very low price.
j ...because he didn't agree with her ideas.

The Bugaboo jacket

LANGUAGE NOTE

Sentence linkers

Look at these ways of linking the different parts of sentences.

Gert decided to run Columbia herself **because** *she needed money to repay her husband's loan;* **but** *she didn't have any management experience, and the company accountant resigned,* **so** *she had a lot of problems at first.*

1 We use *because* and *so* when we want to give the reason for an action or decision. These words can appear in a different position in the sentence.

She decided to run the company **because** *she needed money.* [decision > reason]
Because *she needed money, she decided to run the company.* [reason > decision]
She needed money, **so** *she decided to run the company.* [reason > decision]

2 We use *but* for contrast, when an action or decision is different from what we would normally expect.

She decided to run the company, **but** *she didn't have any management experience.*

3 Normally, we don't begin a sentence with *so*, *but*, or *and.*

D LANGUAGE FOCUS

Fill in the spaces in the sentences with *because, so,* or *but.* The first one is done for you.

1 The company is recruiting 100 new employees this year ...*so*... it is moving to larger offices.
2 We're sending her to the Madrid office .... she speaks good Spanish.
3 The flight was delayed .... he was late for the meeting.
4 The rooms in the hotel were very comfortable .... the food in the hotel restaurant wasn't good.
5 He can't be our new Financial Director .... he isn't a qualified accountant.
6 Last year, sales increased by eight per cent .... profits fell by two per cent.

E PRACTICE

1 How many different ways can you think of to complete this sentence?

I want to learn English	*because*	....
	so	....
	but	....

2 Write some more sentences with *because, so,* and *but.*

9

Dealing with problems

9.1 Making decisions

***Will* or Present Continuous**

I'll go. I'm going.

SEE LANGUAGE FILE: 16

A **READING**

Maria Jarvis works in Frankfurt, Germany. Next Tuesday, she has an appointment in Bristol in the west of England. She wants to travel there on the same day.

With a partner, look at the two timetables and the fax, and plan her journey.

FAX

To: Maria Jarvis

FROM

From: Philip Benn

Dear Maria,

This is to confirm our meeting in Bristol on Tuesday 31st October at 6 p.m.

I suggest that you take a taxi to get from Heathrow Airport to London Paddington station. The journey takes about 45 minutes.

I look forward to seeing you again.

Best regards.

Philip

FROM FRANKFURT TO LONDON HEATHROW

BA = British Airways
LH = Lufthansa

Dep	Arr	Flight
0730	0755	LH4022
0800	0840	BA901
0930	1000	LH4108
1120	1155	BA903
1140	1215	BA903
1330	1400	LH4008
1530	1605	BA905
1730	1800	LH4066
1830	1905	BA909
2130	2200	LH4002

FROM LONDON TO BRISTOL

London Paddington	d1400	1415	1500	1515	1600	1615	1645	1700
Reading	d1420	1441	1526	1541	1626	1641	1711	1726
Didcot Parkway	d —	1455	—	1555	—	—	1726	—
Swindon	a1456	1515	1556	1615	1654	1711	1746	1756
Chippenham	a —	1529	—	1629	—	1725	1800	—
Bath Spa	a —	1542	—	1642	—	1738	1813	
Bristol	a1522	1558	1622	1658	1722	1754	1829	1824

B

LISTENING

Now listen to Maria Jarvis confirming her travel arrangements with her secretary Katya.

1 What plane is Maria taking? And what train?

2 What tense do Maria and Katya use to talk about the future:

a	the Present Simple?	*I fly to London.*
b	the Present Continuous?	*I'm flying to London.*
c	the Future with *will*?	*I'll fly to London.*

Why do they use this tense?

LANGUAGE NOTE

Will for decisions

When we make a decision about what to do in the future, we use *I'll...* (= *I will...*).

There are trains at 4, 5, and 6 o'clock. Which one do you prefer?
***I'll take** the 5 o'clock.*

If our plans are already made, we use the Present Continuous to talk about the future (see also Unit 6, page 75; File 12, page 170).

***What are you doing** next week?*
***I'm attending** the Madrid conference.*

We use *will* when the decision is made at the time of speaking, and we use the Present Continuous when the decision was taken before the time of speaking.

C

LISTENING AND LANGUAGE FOCUS

Maria Jarvis now has another meeting in London next Tuesday at lunchtime. She talks again to Katya about changing her travel arrangements.

1 As you listen, look again at the timetables in A. Which plane and train does Maria decide to take?

2 Now complete these details of her travel arrangements.

Depart Frankfurt at .... by Flight ....

Arrive London Heathrow at ....

Depart London Paddington at ....

Arrive Bristol at ....

3 Maria makes some decisions about what to do. Listen again and complete her words.

K The one before is a Lufthansa flight at half-past nine, arriving at Heathrow at ten o'clock.
M OK. I'll .... on the half-past nine plane.
K Half-past nine. OK. So, that's Flight LH 4108. And what about your train to Bristol?
M Well, I think my meeting in London will .... about three hours.
K So you won't have time to .... the four o'clock train.
M No, I'll .... a .... train. When's the next one?
K There's one at 16.15, another at 16.45, and another at 17.00.
M OK. I'll .... on the 17.00.

D PRACTICE

You are Maria Jarvis. You have some problems with your visit to Bristol next Tuesday. Decide what to do in each case. (You must visit Philip Benn's company – you cannot cancel your meeting.)

1 A client in Frankfurt wants a meeting next Tuesday.
I'll tell him I'm not free on Tuesday.
or *I'll ask him if he's free on Wednesday.*

2 The hotel where you wanted to stay in Bristol is closed for repairs.
3 There aren't any Business Class seats on the flight you want.
4 Your meeting in London for Tuesday lunchtime is cancelled.
5 You hear that Lufthansa are going on strike next Tuesday.
6 Now you hear that British Rail are going on strike next Tuesday!
7 Philip Benn's assistant phones you a day before your departure to say that Philip is ill.
8 You're leaving today. You wake up and look at your alarm clock. Your plane to London left fifteen minutes ago!

E LANGUAGE FOCUS

Will or Present Continuous for future? Decide if the verbs in *italics* are in the correct form. Correct them if necessary.

1 ○ What would you like to drink?
● *I'm having* a whisky, please.
2 ○ Where *are you flying* tomorrow?
● To Rio.
3 ○ I'm sorry, sir, but there are no more seats on this flight.
● That's OK. *I'll take* the next one.
4 ○ What time *will we meet* the Managing Director?
● Our appointment is at 10.00.
5 ○ I can't open this door.
● Wait a second. *I'm opening* it for you.

9.2 Complaining

Complaining and offering help

too / not enough   *Shall I ... ?*   *I'll...*

SEE LANGUAGE FILE: 16

A

VOCABULARY

1 What problems can you have (or have you had) in the following places?

2 Now look at these sentences. Which of the things mentioned in the table could each complaint refer to? Tick (✓) the right boxes. The first one is done for you.

	hotel room	food	wine
a It's too noisy.	✓		
b It's too cold.			
c It isn't cold enough.			
d It's too sweet.			
e It's too small.			
f It's too dear.			
g It's dirty.			
h It isn't big enough.			
i It's stale.			
j It isn't hot enough.			

LANGUAGE NOTE

Too and *not...enough*

Too... and *not...enough* are used with adjectives when you want to say that something is not acceptable.

This restaurant is too expensive. *The service isn't quick enough.*

B

PRACTICE

Re-write the sentences using *too...* or *not...enough*, so that both sentences have the same meaning. The first one is done for you.

1 This room is too noisy.
It *isn't quiet enough.*

2 He's too young to be a hotel manager.
He isn't ....

3 This bed is too short.
It isn't ....

4 The shower isn't hot enough.
It's ....

5 The hotel is too far from the station.
It ....

6 The room is too dark – there's only one 60-watt lamp.
It ....

C

LISTENING

Listen to this dialogue in a restaurant and choose the correct answer.

a The man isn't happy because:
1 the service is slow.
2 the food is bad.

b He asks the waiter to:
1 see what the problem is.
2 change his order.

c The waiter apologizes and says:
1 he will bring the food now.
2 the usual chef is ill.

d The waiter offers the man:
1 a different dish on the menu.
2 another drink.

e The man is:
1 angry.
2 patient.

D

LANGUAGE FOCUS

1 Listen to the restaurant dialogue again. Notice how the expressions below are used.

Excuse me, but…

I'm sorry about that.

Could you… ?

I'll…

Thank you.

I'm afraid… .
Shall I… ?

Yes, please.
or
No, thank you.

2 With a partner, practise the restaurant dialogue using the notes above. Look at the Tapescript to check your answers.

LANGUAGE NOTE

Offering to do something

1 We can use *I'll…* (= *I will*) to offer to do, or promise to do, something.

I'm still waiting for my meal.
I'm sorry about that. I'll go and check in the kitchen.

2 We use *Shall I… ?* when we offer to do something, and we want an answer from the other person.

Shall I bring you another drink?
Yes, please.

E

SPEAKING

With a partner, practise dialogues for the following situations.

1 You're in a hotel. The bedroom window doesn't open and it's very hot. Talk to the receptionist.
2 You're in a bar. Your glass is dirty and the beer is too warm. Talk to the barman.
3 You're leaving your hotel. The bill is 20% more than you thought. Talk to the manager.
4 You're in a restaurant. You are sitting next to the kitchen. Waiters are coming in and out all the time and there's a lot of noise. Talk to your waiter.

F

VOCABULARY

1 Match sentences 1-11 with the corresponding replies (a-k).

1 Excuse me. My luggage wasn't on the conveyor belt.
2 I think there's a mistake in my bill.
3 Excuse me. My room is freezing cold.
4 I think you gave me the wrong change.
5 I'm sorry, but I've just spilt wine on the tablecloth.
6 Excuse me. I can't find the car in Lot 25.
7 Waiter. Excuse me. This steak isn't cooked enough.
8 I'm still waiting for my clean laundry. Where is it?
9 I'm sorry, but I can't find my room key.
10 Look! I didn't ask you to show me all the sights!
11 I'm afraid I don't have any small change for a tip.

a Yes. I'm afraid we have a little problem with the central heating.
b I told you before, it's number **thirty**-five.
c Sorry about that. You're right. It's \$52, not \$520.
d Well, you'll have to pay for a new one if you've lost it.
e I'm sorry, sir, but it's the quickest way at this time of day.
f Could you wait a moment? I'll just check with the baggage handlers.
g No, I didn't. Count it again.
h Don't worry, Madam, these things happen. I'll move you to another table.
i It doesn't matter, sir. I accept banknotes.
j I'm terribly sorry. I'll ring and see what's happening.
k Well, if you wanted it well done, why didn't you ask before?

2 Some of the expressions used above are impolite. Which ones? How could you make them more polite?

9.3 Thinking ahead

***Will* for prediction**

I think we will. *I don't think we will.*

SEE LANGUAGE FILE: 16

A **READING**

Maria Jarvis exports electrical goods. She is in Bristol to present a new product to Philip Benn, a British distributor.

1 Look at the picture and the product description. How is the YB 206 different from a normal radio?

The Yacht Boy® 206

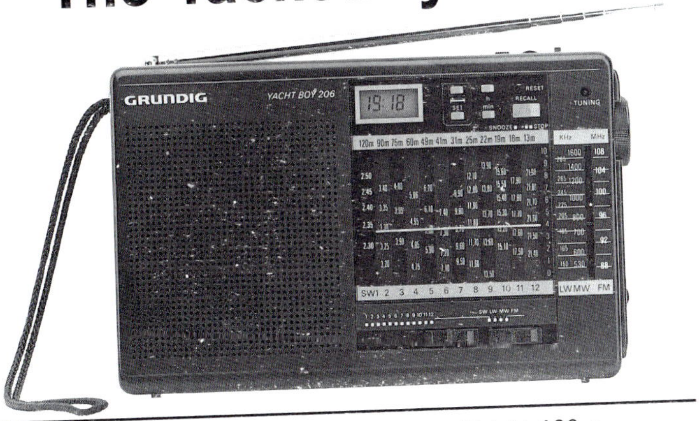

★ *Dimensions 18 cm x 11 cm x 4 cm* ★ *Weight 420 g*
★ *15-band radio: FM, MW and LW, and 12 shortwave bands*
★ *Telescopic antenna* ★ *Digital clock* ★ *Alarm clock*
★ *"Sleep" function: switches off automatically after 10-60 minutes*
★ *Mono headphones*

2 Match an expression on the left (a-e) with one on the right (1-5) which means the opposite.

a	It's difficult to carry.	1	It's light.
b	It has many features.	2	It's very basic.
c	It's state-of-the-art.	3	It comes with headphones.
d	It's heavy.	4	It's old-fashioned.
e	There are no accessories.	5	It's portable.

3 Which of these expressions would you use to describe the YB 206?

B

LISTENING

1 Look at the three lists below and answer these questions.

a Who do you think will be the best customers for the YB 206?
b Where will it sell?
c What will be the best way to advertise?

The YB 206 – Marketing Suggestions

Customers?	Sales outlets?	Advertising?
• business people	• supermarkets	• business magazines
• people living abroad	• mail order	• general magazines
• general public	• airport gift shops	• direct mailing

2 Now listen to Maria Jarvis telling Philip Benn about future markets for the YB 206. Which of the suggestions in the list above does she mention? Put a tick (✓) next to the suggestion if she recommends it, and a cross (✗) if she doesn't.

3 Listen again and complete these extracts from the dialogue.

EXTRACT 1

PB OK. So business people working abroad .... buy it. What about people *living* abroad?
MJ Yes, I'm sure .... be interested. But you .... sell many to the general public, I'm afraid.
PB So, as far as sales outlets are concerned, supermarkets are no good.
MJ No. I'm sure that supermarkets .... be interested in it. It's too specialized, and the price is too high. But I think you .... have customers in airport gift shops.

EXTRACT 2

MJ But you'll get a lot of orders if you .... in *business* magazines. And direct mailing is the best way to target residents abroad.
PB OK, Maria. So, when do I have to make a .... ?
MJ As soon as possible!
PB I was afraid you'd say that!
MJ No, seriously. My client wants a UK distributor as soon as possible. If you .... make a decision now, you probably .... have another chance later.

LANGUAGE NOTE

Other uses of *will*

1 We use *will* when we want to make predictions about the future.

I think we will sell a lot in Europe in the next five years.
I don't think we will advertise in newspapers next year.

2 *Will* often abbreviates to *-'ll* after personal pronouns, in spoken and written English. *(I'll, you'll, he'll, she'll, it'll, we'll, they'll).*

Will not usually abbreviates to *won't.*

3 Notice the construction in sentences with *if.*

If + Present Simple + *will/won't*
If you wait until tomorrow, you won't have enough time.
If you don't buy it now, you'll have problems later.

C

PRACTICE

1 How will the world be different in 25 years' time? Make predictions about the following. Give your reasons, where possible. A suggested answer for 1 is given.

1 Europe — top economic power
I don't think Europe will be the top economic power, because Asian countries are growing much more quickly.

2 plane travel — less expensive — rail travel
3 more people — work part-time
4 computer — in every home
5 all cars — electric

2 Now make some other predictions and discuss them with a partner. Do you agree?

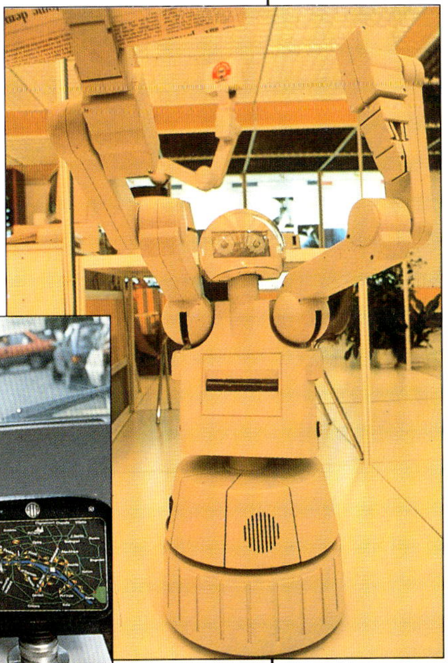

D

PRACTICE

You work for a British company. Read this message from your boss.

An important American client is coming tomorrow - Mr Dooley from AMK. I'm afraid I can't meet him because I'm playing in the final of a golf tournament. Can you see him for me?
I think he's ready to sign a new contract, so I don't think there'll be any problems. He's a difficult man, but quite nice really!
Thanks
Bob

What will you say or do in the following situations? Make sentences with *If...* . The first one is done for you.

a Mr Dooley asks to see your boss.
If he asks to see my boss, I'll say that he's ill.
b He doesn't understand your English.
c He asks you to show him round your factory again.
d He says that your competitors are cheaper.
e He asks for a discount.
f You go to a restaurant, and he doesn't like the food.
g He decides to wait another two weeks before signing the contract.
h He suggests a game of golf after lunch at your boss's golf club.
i He offers you a job in his company.

E

PRONUNCIATION

In Unit 6.3 (page 84) we saw how a word beginning with *a, e, i, o, u,* or *y* is usually linked with the end of the preceding word when we speak quickly.

I'll pass on the message as soon as I see him.

1 Mark all the linked words in these sentences.

a I'll do it if I can.

b If you can't answer the question, I'll ask another person.

c I don't think I'll advertise in a business magazine.

d If we have a game of tennis, we won't arrive on time.

e I think you'll sell a lot in airports.

2 Now listen and repeat. Check your answers.

9.4 Apologizing

Written and spoken apologies

We would like to apologize... *Sorry about...*

SEE LANGUAGE FILES: 7, 8, 16

A SPEAKING

1 When you or your company has done something wrong, what are the best ways to apologize?

a a personal visit
b a phone call
c a letter

2 Which kind of apology do you prefer to make? And which kind do you prefer to receive?

3 Which ways of apologizing are most common, in your experience?

B LISTENING

Philip Benn distributes electrical goods in Europe. There is a call for him from a client.

1 Listen to the first call and complete the memorandum.

BENN DISTRIBUTION LTD
CUSTOMER SERVICE DEPARTMENT

MEMORANDUM

Date .... Message taken by ....
Caller .... Company ....
Model .... Order N° ....
Quantity ....

Problem ....
....

Action ....
....

2 Philip Benn calls back. Listen to the second call and answer the questions.

a What was the cause of the problem?
b What two things does Philip Benn promise to do?

C

PAIR WORK

Have telephone conversations with your partner. There are two situations.

Person A: Your information is in File L page 160.
Person B: Your information is below.

1 You are Mr Bush, Accounts Manager of SIMCO.

a A client phones you. They have a problem with an invoice. Ask them for the invoice number and date. Say you'll look into the problem and ask when you can call them back.
b Call them back. Apologize, the invoice is for £5,000, not £6,000. It was a computer error. Promise to send a new invoice today.

2 You are Simon Richards. You ordered 150 glasses from Valio Inc. three weeks ago, but you never received them.

a Call Mr Geraldo, Production Manager of Valio Inc. Explain the problem and ask him to look into it.
b Mr Geraldo phones you back. He will ask you for your address: it's 2017 East River Drive, Huntsville, Alabama.

D

READING

Mr Carlton, manager of a gift shop at Heathrow Airport, receives some RK 529 calculators without instruction manuals.

1 Below is the customer's fax **and** the reply from Philip Benn. The two faxes are all mixed up. Put the sentences in the right order, using the table opposite. The first ones are done for you.

a We will send ten copies of the instruction manual to you today.
b We received delivery this morning of ten of your RK529 calculators.
c Thank you for your fax of 25th June.
d When I opened the package, I saw that there was no instruction manual in the boxes.
e We thank you for your patience, and look forward to receiving your next order.
f We want to sell these calculators during the busy summer period,
g Dear Mr Benn,
h Dear Mr Carlton,
i This was due to an error in packing.
j Please could you give this matter your immediate attention.
k I look forward to hearing from you.
l We would like to apologize for the mistake in delivery.
m In addition, we will be pleased to offer you a discount of 5% off your next order.
n ... so I would be grateful if you could send me the missing instruction manual in the next few days.

Mr Carlton's fax	Philip Benn's reply
g	*h*

2 With a partner, make a list of expressions from the two faxes which you could use to write similar complaints and apologies.

E

LANGUAGE FOCUS

The language of business letters is usually more formal than telephone language.

1 Look at these phrases from the telephone dialogues in B. What phrases in the two faxes above are used to say the same thing? The first one is done for you.

Telephone dialogue	Business letters/faxes
1 They arrived this morning.	*We received delivery this morning.*
2 Could you look into the problem?	
3 Could you send me... ?	
4 Can you call me back?	
5 Sorry about the mistake.	
6 We'll give you a discount.	

2 Can you think of any examples of differences between business letters and telephoning in your language?

10

People at work

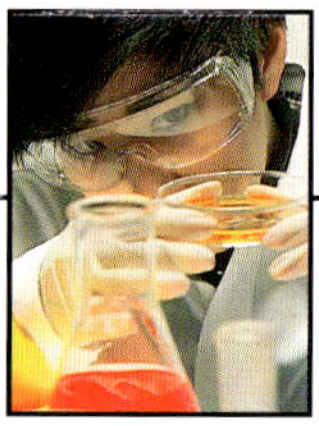

10.1 Suggesting and recommending

Language of suggestions

We should... What about... ? Why don't we... ?

SEE LANGUAGE FILE: 18

LISTENING

In 1986, two young property surveyors, Julian Metcalfe and Sinclair Beecham, were in a café in central London. One of them had an idea for a new business.

1 Listen to their conversation and number the following suggestions in the order you hear them:

	order	yes/no
look in the newspaper for premises		
open a sandwich shop	*1*	*yes*
only use fresh ingredients		
play classical music in the shop		
have very high prices		
make an appointment with the bank manager		
import bread from France		
play pop music in the shop		

2 Now listen again, and complete the second column. Write *yes* if they think the idea is good, and *no* if it is not a good idea.

B

LANGUAGE FOCUS

Here are some expressions used for making suggestions.

We should...
I don't think we should...
How about .... -ing... ?
What about .... -ing... ?
Why don't we... ?

Look at the Tapescript for A (page 184) and underline the suggestion expressions.

We should open a sandwich shop.
What about importing bread from France?

C

PRACTICE

Julian Metcalfe and Sinclair Beecham opened their first *Pret a Manger* sandwich shop. Now they have over thirty shops in London (including one at Heathrow Airport), and annual sales of £11m.

What do you think they should do now, and why?

I think they should *I don't think they should*	*open more shops* *sell the business* *increase their prices by 20%* *develop new products* *advertise on television* *create new management positions* *open shops abroad*	*because...*

LANGUAGE NOTE

Recommending action

1 We use *should* for recommending action.

I think we ***should*** *import bread from France.*

2 In the negative form, we say *I don't think we should...* (not ~~*I think we shouldn't...*~~)

I don't think we should *play pop music in the shop.*

3 *Should* is used when you have a strong opinion about something. If you want to make a less strong suggestion, you can use these expressions.

Why don't *we make an appointment with the bank manager?*

How about
What about *playing classical music?*

D

PRACTICE

You and your partner are managers in the same company. You have a number of problems.

1 One solution is suggested for each problem. Think of some more.

problem	suggested solution	other solutions
A new competitor, BRP, took 5% of your market share last year.	Reduce your prices.	
Your main supplier, TFD West, often delivers late (but their prices are the lowest in town).	Find a new supplier.	
The best candidate for the post of Personnel Manager is a woman, but she is expecting a baby in four months' time.	Employ her.	
Not enough staff are using the company canteen; many of them are buying sandwiches in *Pret a Manger*!	Close the canteen.	

2 Now discuss each problem, following these guidelines.

Managing Director

Explain the problem and ask for a solution.

What do you think we should do?

Financial Director

Suggest a solution and give a reason.

I think we should... because...

Managing Director

Reject the idea and give a reason.

I don't think we should... because...

Suggest another solution.

Why don't we.../How about... ?

Financial Director

Accept or reject the suggestion.

I agree.../I don't agree... because...

E

ROLE PLAY

Work in groups.

Your teacher/boss is leaving the school/company after fifteen years of service. You want to buy him or her a present.

What are his/her interests? How much do you want to spend?

With your partners, suggest five possible presents, and then agree on which one to buy. Use the language of recommending and suggesting.

F

SPEAKING

1 In your country, what presents or gifts do you normally give to:

a someone who is retiring from your company?
b your host and hostess when you are invited for dinner at their house?
c a foreign client who is visiting your company (and country) for the first time?

2 What present would you like from your company when you retire? What **wouldn't** you like?

3 What sort of gifts do people usually give in your company/country? How is it different in other companies/countries you know?

10.2 Job responsibilities

Obligation and permission

must, have to, can, can't, mustn't, don't have to

SEE LANGUAGE FILE: 17

A READING AND SPEAKING

Read the text and answer the questions that follow.

Jacqueline Roy is a Personnel Manager at Ecospar, the Dutch chemicals company. She is also the mother of three young children. She is very happy with her job conditions, because she **has to** work only four days a week. She **can** also bring her children to work because Ecospar has good childcare facilities. Obviously she **can't** see them during the day because she is so busy. But she **doesn't have to** work at weekends, and this makes family life much easier for her. To be accepted as a woman in a man's world, she believes she **must** do her job better than the men around her, especially as she chooses to work part time. Her advice to working women: 'You **mustn't** be too nice.'

1 Which of the verbs in **bold** mean:

a it is necessary for her to do it? .... or ....
b it is possible for her to do it? ....
c it isn't necessary for her to do it? ....
d it isn't possible to do it? .... or ....

2 Now complete these sentences about Jacqueline Roy using the verbs in **1** above. The first one is done for you.

a She ...*can*... be with her children at weekends.
b She only works four days a week, so she .... work on Fridays.
c She .... send her children to a nursery because there are childcare facilities at Ecospar.
d She .... work very hard to be accepted by male colleagues.
e She thinks working women .... be tough.

3 In pairs or groups, discuss the following questions.

a What do you think of Jacqueline Roy's working arrangements? Do similar arrangements exist in your company/country?

b Jacqueline Roy says that working women 'mustn't be too nice'. Do you agree with her advice?

LANGUAGE NOTE

Obligation and permission

It's possible.	*We can...* *Can we... ?*	It isn't possible.	*We can't...* *We mustn't...*
It's necessary.	*We have to...* *We must...* *Do we have to... ?* *Must we... ?*	It isn't necessary.	*We don't have to...*

B PRACTICE

Talk about your own job, using the expressions below:

I have to... / must... / don't have to... / can... / can't... / mustn't...

...work long hours.
...visit clients.
...be late for work.
...wear a suit at work.
...answer the telephone.
...smoke at work.
...choose my working hours.
...take my holidays in the summer (or winter).
...speak English in the company.
...be the first to get to work.
...entertain visitors to the company.
...write (or read) letters and reports in English.

C LANGUAGE FOCUS

1 Where would you see these signs? (For example, 2 – *In a library*)

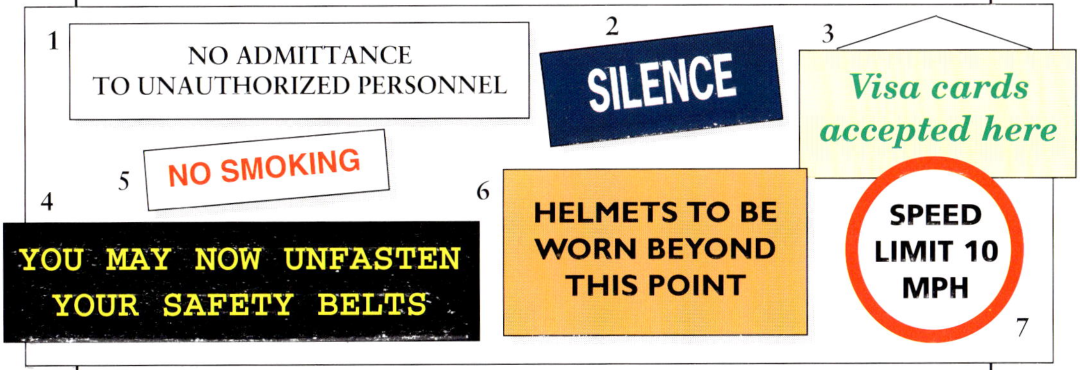

2 What do the signs mean? Use the verbs in the Language Note. (For example, 1 SILENCE = *You mustn't talk.*)

D

SPEAKING AND LISTENING

Brian Sullivan

Emi Ishikawa

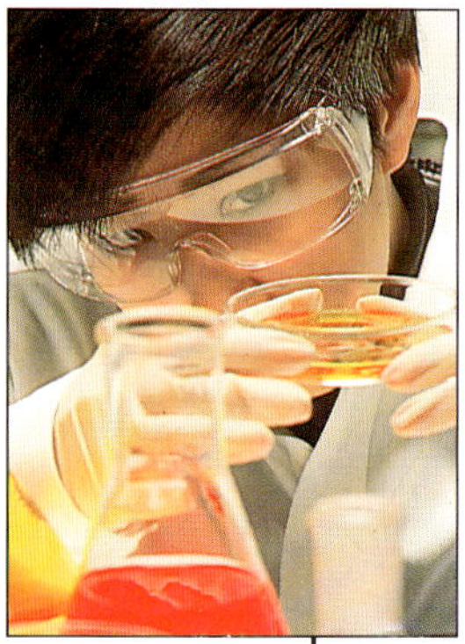

Leif Olsen

Anne Redcar

Anna Hardcastle

1 Look at the five people above. What are their jobs? Choose from this list.

a scientist
b secretary
c accountant
d security guard
e export sales manager

2 What does each person have to do in his or her job?

3 Listen to three of these people answering questions about their jobs. Who is talking in each case? What are the words and phrases that helped you to decide?

E

PAIR WORK

What's my job?

Person A: Choose a job that interests you (it could be one of the jobs in D). Don't tell your partner. He or she must guess what the job is by asking you questions.

Person B: You must find out your partner's job. Ask him or her questions. You can use B and the interviews in D for ideas.

Do you have to... ?
Can you... ?
When/what/where do you have to... ?
When/where can you... ?

Obviously, you **mustn't** ask direct questions like: ~~*What do you do?*~~ or ~~*What is your job?*~~

10.3 Correcting information

Contrastive stress

No, not thir<u>teen</u>; <u>thir</u>ty.

SEE LANGUAGE FILE: 18

A

READING AND LISTENING

1 Look at the photo and the Fact File. What do you know about Pilar Almeida?

FACT FILE

Name: Pilar Almeida
Age: 43
Employer: Cygnus S.A.
Position: Managing Director
Number of employees: 500
Number of women senior managers: One (Pilar Almeida)
Company products: Software systems
Clients: Smaller companies in Spain and abroad
Education: Degree in Business Science (University of Madrid)
Joined company: 1977
First management job: 1979
Became Managing Director: 1990

2 A reporter is interviewing Pilar Almeida on a radio programme called *In Business*. Some of the information in the Fact File is not right. Listen and correct it.

3 Pilar Almeida corrects the reporter several times. Listen again. What words does she use?

a Thank you very much. In fact, I'm .... forty- .... years old, I'm forty- ....

b ○ And you got your first management post two years later?
● No, ... It was .... years later, in 1980.

c ○ Yes, it says here that Cygnus has about 500 employees.
● No, that's not .... We have nearly .... hundred, not .... hundred.

4 Which words does Pilar stress? Why?

LANGUAGE NOTE
Correcting information

1 Here are some different expressions we use to correct information.

No, that's not quite right.
No, not exactly.
No. In fact...

2 Don't use this expression: it sounds impolite.

No, you're wrong!

3 When we are correcting factual information, we stress (a) the word that is correct, and (b) the word that is incorrect.

○ *She's forty-three years old.*
● *No. In fact she's forty-**seven**.*
*No, that's not quite right. Not forty-**three**, forty-**seven**.*
*No, not exactly. She's forty-**seven**, not forty-**three**.*
*No, she isn't forty-**three**, she's forty-**seven**.*

B

LANGUAGE FOCUS

1 Listen to the different ways of correcting information in the Language Note above. Repeat the example sentences.

2 Now look again at the Fact File in A, and correct the following statements. Try all the different ways of correcting information given in the Language Note.

a She joined the company in 1987.
b She studied Computer Science.
c I think the company makes electrical systems.
d There are three women senior managers at Cygnus.
e Cygnus sells its products to large companies.
f She studied at the University of Salamanca.

C

PRACTICE

Correct the information in these sentences, as in the example below.

○ *Oh, so you're English!*
● *No, I'm not English. In fact, I'm Spanish.*

1 So, you work for C&A.
2 I understand you're learning French at the moment.
3 I think banks in this country open at 7 a.m.

4 You've got eight children, I believe.
5 George Bush was the American President before Ronald Reagan.
6 So, you're from Russia.
7 I think Kennedy died in 1966.
8 If I remember correctly, you joined your company a year ago.
9 I understand you're taking ten weeks holiday this year.

D

ROLE PLAY

Person A: Look at File K, page 159.

Person B: There are two situations.

1 You are Mr/s Brearly. Last week, you phoned the Plaza Hotel in Brighton to reserve a double room with bath for four nights from the 13th April. You asked for half board (breakfast and evening meal), and a room with a view of the sea.
Now you receive a phone call from the hotel (Person A).

2 You are Martin(a) Solomon of ASTA Plastics. When you got to work this morning there was a fax on your desk from Mr/Ms Dobson of Artlife Creations. It says that they took delivery of an order from you yesterday and there were several mistakes. Phone Mrs Dobson and read the order information you have to her.
Correct the mistakes in your version.

ASTA PLASTICS

Despatch Department

Client: ARTLIFE.......... Date of order: 12/5...

Product code	Description	Quantity
146/98	PICTURE FRAMES-RED	150
146/58	PICTURE FRAMES-BLUE	150
351/74	PLASTIC COVERS	500
564/99	250 cm TUBES	80

11

Getting a job

11.1 Job advertisements

Job application vocabulary

hard-working *ambitious* *dynamic*

A

SPEAKING

Here are some different jobs.

a Who earns the most? Who earns the least?
b Which is the most interesting job?
c Which job has the most responsibility?
d Which job would you prefer to do? Why?

4 teacher

1 research scientist

2 lawyer

3 engineer

5 secretary

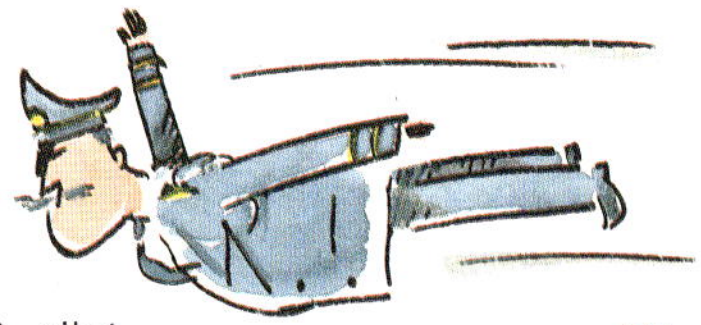

6 pilot

8 accountant

7 doctor

9 salesperson

B

PRACTICE

1 Look at the adjectives below. Match each of the definitions (a-g) with one of the adjectives. The first one is done for you.

calm	outgoing	punctual
ambitious	practical	dynamic
sensitive	persuasive	good with figures
patient	reliable	good with words
precise	hard-working	energetic

Definitions:

a someone who wants to get to the top *ambitious*
b someone who thinks of other people's feelings
c someone who doesn't panic
d someone who rarely makes mistakes
e someone who you can trust or count on
f someone who can change people's opinions
g someone who is good at finding solutions to problems

2 Now match the adjectives in **1** with the jobs in A. Make sentences like this:

An accountant must be good with figures.

LANGUAGE NOTE

What's he like?

When asking someone to describe a person, we often use the expression:
What's he/she like?

This can be a request for a physical description of the person.
She's tall with long fair hair.
He's short and dark, and has a moustache and beard.

Or, it can be a request for a description of their personality.

What's your boss like? | *She's very nice.*
He's a bit lazy.
She's very patient.

C

SPEAKING

1 How do you describe people in your own language? Think of words you use to describe people's appearance and personality. Can you translate them into English?

2 Think of two people: one you admire and one you dislike. Describe them to your partner. Now listen to your partner's descriptions.

D READING

Luis Antonio de Oliveira works for a research institute in Rio de Janeiro. The institute organizes drug trials for pharmaceutical companies. The trials are to test drugs for safety before they come on the market. Luis sees this advertisement in the newspapers.

1 Read the advertisement and answer the questions as quickly as possible.

MARKETING MANAGER (SOUTH AMERICA)
for a
Leading International Pharmaceutical Company

Salary: $80-95,000 + car + full medical insurance

Are you hard-working, ambitious, and dynamic?
Do you enjoy a challenge?

We are looking for a **qualified doctor** with sales and marketing experience to be responsible for promotion of our range of antibiotics in South America.

The position is based in São Paulo (Brazil).

Languages: Portuguese, English, and Spanish
Experience: At least three years in medicine + five years in the industry

Apply to: Mrs Joy Gilbert
Personnel Department
AVRC
P.O. Box 2435
London W1AA 6WW

a What is the job?
b What is the salary?
c Where is the job?
d What is the name of the company?
e What kind of company is it?
f What qualities is the company looking for?

2 What other information do you think Luis needs before he decides whether to apply for the job? With a partner, make a list.

E

VOCABULARY

Complete the paragraph using the words below.

short list	post/position	apply
offer	CV (*Am. English:* resumé)	advertisement
interview	application	candidate

Luis decides to .... (1) for the job. He has to send his .... (2) and a letter of .... (3) to the address given on the .... (4) . If he is a good .... (5), he will be put on a .... (6) and invited for an .... (7). If he is successful, they will .... (8) him the .... (9).

F

WRITING

With a partner, prepare a job advertisement for one of the jobs below. Your advertisement must include: the salary, the age and type of person you want, and anything else you decide is important.

1 mining engineers to work in gold mines in South Africa
2 young people to work as tour guides in South-East Asia
3 a salesperson for a company manufacturing office equipment

11.2 Applying for a job

The Present Perfect tense

for *since*

SEE LANGUAGE FILES: 3, 14

A

READING

You are Joy Gilbert, Personnel Officer of AVRC. Read Luis's letter of application and answer the questions in your manager's memo.

Luis Antonio de Oliveira
53, rua Maria Angelica
22461 Rio de Janeiro
Brazil

Joy Gilbert
A V R C
P.O.Box 2435
London W1AA 6WW

Attn. Joy Gilbert

22 June 199x

Ref. Advertisement Sunday Times.

Dear Ms. Gilbert,

I am writing in response to your advertisement for a Marketing Manager in last week's *Sunday Times*. I am 39 years old, Brazilian, with a medical degree from the University of São Paulo, and an MBA from the University of California, Los Angeles. I qualified as a Medical Doctor in 1982 and graduated from U.C.L.A. in 1988. I speak fluent English and Portuguese, and have a good knowledge of Spanish.

I have worked for Medilab here in Rio since 1992. I am in charge of clinical trials for new antibiotics. I have experience of the pharmaceutical industry with Schering Plough, where I spent two years, and Merck (eighteen months).

Before I started my two-year MBA course (1986-1988), I worked in Peru for a medical charity.

I am keen to find a position which combines my experience of marketing and medicine, and I would particularly like to work with an international company. I got married in 1991 and we now have two children, but we are happy to move overseas. My wife works as a nurse, so she can move easily.

I am hard-working, independent, and enjoy a challenge. I can provide full references if necessary. Please find enclosed my resumé.

Yours truly,

Luis Antonio de Oliveira

INTERNAL MEMORANDUM

To: Joy Gilbert (Personnel Officer)
From: Alan Green (Personnel Manager)
Date: 24 June
Re: Marketing Manager (South America)

When you look at the applications for the Marketing Manager job we advertised this week, please can you make notes on these questions:

1) Where do they live? (We need someone local.)
2) How old are they? (Sorry, but I don't want anyone over forty.)
3) Do they have the right sort of work experience?
4) What does their wife or husband do? (Can they move quickly?)
5) Why do they want to change jobs?
6) What are they like, in your opinion?

We'll look at the applications together tomorrow.

LANGUAGE NOTE

The Present Perfect

1 We use the Present Perfect to talk about an action or event in the past which is unfinished.

He has lived in Rio since 1992. (He still lives there.)
He has been married since 1991. (He is still married.)
How long has he worked for Medilab?
He has worked for Medilab for three years. (He still works for Medilab.)

2 We use *since* with a moment in time.
since 1992, since June, since two o'clock

We use *for* with a period of time.
for seven years, for a month, for half an hour

He has been married since 1991. (moment)
He has worked in Brazil for four years. (period)

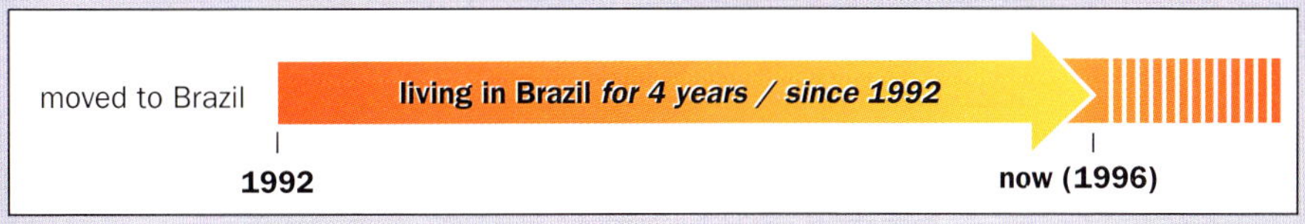

B

LANGUAGE FOCUS

Look back at Luis's letter and complete the missing questions and answers.

1	How long .... ?	He has lived in Rio ....
2	How long .... ?	He worked for Schering for two years.
3	How long .... ?	He got married in 1991.
4	When .... ?	He got his MBA in 1988.
5	When was he born?	He ....
6	How long .... ?	He has been a doctor since 1977.

C

PRACTICE AND QUESTION-MAKING

Sometimes we can say the same thing in different ways. Look at this example.

He has worked for the company for two years.
He joined the company two years ago.

1 Re-write these sentences with the words provided. The first one is done for you.

a She has been married for two years. (get married / ago)
She got married two years ago.
b It's eleven o'clock and I've been here since nine. (arrive / ago)
c We bought the house five years ago. (own / for five years)
d She became Sales Director in 1993. (be / since)
e I got my car in 1994. (have / for)

2 Now make questions for each of the sentences in **1**.

a *When did she get married?*
b ....
c ....
d ....
e ....

D

LISTEN AND REPLY

Listen and reply in a natural way. There are ten questions.

E

PRACTICE

Correct these sentences.

1 I work for IBM. In fact, I work for them for twenty years.
2 I have worked for Glaxo for ten years and then I got a job at BMS.
3 Our present chairman was chairman for ten years.
4 I have joined the company in 1985.
5 The company is based in Swindon since 1989.
6 I have worked in research since ten years.

F

PAIR WORK

Person A: Your information is in File P, page 161.

Person B: Look at Luis's CV. Some of the information is missing. Ask Person A for the missing information and answer Person A's questions.

Name	Luis Antonio DE OLIVEIRA
Date of Birth	....
Place of Birth	Santa Rosa, Brazil
Nationality	Brazilian
Address	53, rua Maria Angelica 22461 Rio de Janeiro, Brazil
Phone	....
Marital Status	Married, two children (aged ...... and ......). Married 1991

EMPLOYMENT HISTORY

1992-present	**Medilab, Rio de Janeiro.** Responsible for Clinical Trials (Antibiotics)
1990-92	**Merck, Buenos Aires.** Assistant Marketing Manager.
19......-90	**Schering Plough,** New Jersey, USA. Product Manager.
1982-86	**Médecins Sans Frontières, Peru.** Project Manager, Vaccination Programs.

EDUCATION

1986-88	U.C.L.A., ... USA Masters in Business Administration. (Major: Sales and Marketing)
1975-82	Medical School. Graduated 1982 cum laude.
19......-74	Vasco da Gama High School, São Paulo

INTERESTS

astronomy, entomology, hang-gliding, football.

Clean Driving Licence

G

SPEAKING

1 Do you think Luis has written a good letter of application and CV? Are there any things you would like to change?

2 In pairs, make lists of information you would include in a letter of application and CV.

Make your lists under these headings:

A letter of application *A CV*	*must include...* *can include...* *doesn't have to include...* *mustn't include...*

11.3 The interview

Present Perfect tense for questions

Have you ever…?

SEE LANGUAGE FILES: 7, 14

A PRACTICE

1 In a job interview, the interviewers try to find out about interesting things that the candidate has done. Ask other people in the class if they have done the things in the list below (a-f). If they have, ask when.

a travel abroad for more than a month
Have you ever travelled abroad for more than a month?

b study a language abroad
c speak in public
d meet someone famous
e visit Africa
f do a parachute jump

2 Now choose some other things to ask about.

LANGUAGE NOTE

Present Perfect or Past Simple?

1 When talking about events that happened at an unspecified time in the past, we use the Present Perfect. Often, we use the word *ever* in questions to make it clear that we're only interested in **whether** someone has done something, not when they did it.

Have you ever visited Madrid?

2 When we ask or talk about a specific time, we change to the Past Simple.

● *Have you ever worked in South America?*	Present Perfect
○ *Yes, I have.*	Present Perfect
● *When did you work there?*	Past Simple
○ *Last year. I worked for a mining company in Peru.*	Past Simple

B

LISTENING

Luis Antonio de Oliveira is invited for an interview in London.

1 Listen to the first part of the interview and answer the questions.

a Who is Alan Green?
b Why is Luis looking for another job?
c What is Luis's wife's job?
d What is his present salary package?
e What salary is he looking for in the future?
f What languages can he speak?

2 Listen again and complete these sentences.

a ○ I see .... Medilab at the moment. How long .... ?
● .... 1990.

b ○ .... abroad?
● Yes. I .... the States for two years, and in Argentina for a year and a half.

c ○ So, what languages can you speak?
● Portuguese is my .... I can also speak English, Spanish, and a little Italian.

C

PRONUNCIATION

Normally, the word *can* is not stressed. It is pronounced /kən/.
What languages can you speak?
I can speak Portuguese, English, and Spanish.

When *can* is stressed (for example, in short replies) it is pronounced /kæn/.
Can you speak Japanese? Yes, I can.

Can't is always stressed, and is pronounced /kɑːnt/.
No, I can't speak Japanese, I'm afraid.

Now listen to these five sentences and decide which word is said in each case. Complete the table.

	can (unstressed)	*can* (stressed)	*can't*
1	☐	☐	☐
2	☐	☐	☐
3	☐	☐	☐
4	☐	☐	☐
5	☐	☐	☐

D

LISTENING

Luis's interview comes to an end.

1 Listen to the expressions Mr Green uses to end the interview. Tick (✓) the one you hear.

a ☐ I think we'll call it a day.
  ☐ I think I'll call in a day.

b ☐ Is there anything else before you go?
  ☐ Is there anything else you need to know?

c ☐ We'll meet for lunch very soon.
  ☐ I'll be in touch very soon.

d ☐ It was a real pleasure meeting you.
  ☐ I had a real pleasure to meet you.

e ☐ Have a safe travel back.
  ☐ Have a safe journey back.

2 Which of the expressions (a-e) above means:

1 'I enjoyed talking to you.' *d*
2 'It's time to end the interview.'
3 'I hope you don't have any problems travelling home.'
4 'I will contact you soon.'
5 'Do you have any more questions?'

E

READING AND WRITING

A few days later Luis receives a letter from Alan Green.

AVRC

P.O.BOX 2435
LONDON W1AA 6WW

Luis Antonio de Oliveira
53, rua Maria Angelica
22461 Rio de Janeiro
BRAZIL

6th July 19xx

Dear Mr de Oliveira,

Thank you very much for coming to see us in London the day before yesterday. We were very impressed with your interview and would like to offer you the position of Marketing Manager (Antibiotics) for South America. We would like you to start in three months' time.

After a one-year period, we expect to see our market share grow. We are sure you can help us to achieve this.

The starting salary will be $85,000 p.a. plus car and full medical insurance. In the second year, this will rise to $90,000. You will also receive regular profit shares based on sales figures for your area.

If you would like to accept this offer, please contact me at the above address and we will draw up a contract.

I look forward to hearing from you.

Yours sincerely

Alan Green

Alan Green
Human Resources Manager.

1 Mark these statements true (T) or false (F).

a ☐ Luis got the job for a one-year period.
b ☐ Alan Green promises Luis a $5,000 pay rise in a year's time.
c ☐ Luis will receive shares in the company.
d ☐ Luis must start immediately.
e ☐ The contract is enclosed.

2 You are Luis. Send a letter to Alan Green replying to AVRC's job offer.

12

Working in the nineties

12.1 Changing careers

Review of verb tenses

past, present, and future

SEE LANGUAGE FILES: 11-16

A **READING AND SPEAKING**

1 Read the text, and choose the correct verb form *in italics*.

THE CHANGING FACE OF WORK

In the 70s and 80s, most managers *expected/have expected* (1) to continue working until retirement at sixty or sixty-five. But now, the situation *changed/is changing* (2). Since the beginning of the 1990s, many managers in their forties and fifties *lost/have lost* (3) their jobs.

Sometimes, the reason for making managers redundant is a company buy-out or restructuring. Also, the recession of the late 1980s and early 1990s *caused/has caused* (4) many redundancies. But it is also true that fixed-term contracts *becomes/are becoming* (5) more popular, and many companies *prefer/are preferring* (6) younger managers.

The result is that large numbers of unemployed managers *are still looking/still look* (7) for work now. And, for those who are over fifty years old, it's not certain that they *are finding/will find* (8) full-time employment again.

What can a manager *does/do* (9) in this situation? One important lesson is that every manager must be ready for change. You know that you *go/are going* (10) to the office tomorrow morning, but you can't be certain that your job *will exist/is existing* (11) a year from now ●

2 Discuss the following questions in pairs or groups.

a Does the situation described in the article exist in your country?
b Do you agree with the advice given at the end of the article?
c Can you think of any other advice?

LANGUAGE NOTE

Tense review

These are the tenses you have studied in this book.

Name	Use	Example
Present Simple	regular/repeated actions or situations	*I work for IBM.* *He travels to work by train.*
Present Continuous	present actions taking place now	*The phone is ringing.* *He's looking for a new job.*
	future arrangements	*I'm arriving next Monday.*
Future with *will*	predictions	*I think he will lose his job.*
	decisions	*I think I'll go home now.*
Past Simple	finished past actions	*I studied Law for two years.* *I joined ICL two years ago.*
Present Perfect	unfinished past actions	*I've worked here since 1990.* *She's lived here for ten years.*

B

LANGUAGE FOCUS

Complete the questions, using an appropriate form of the verb in brackets. Look carefully at the answers first.

1 Where *are* you *going* ? (go)
I'm going for lunch. It's 12 o'clock.

2 What .... you .... ? (do)
I work in Sales.

3 Why .... you .... to Madrid yesterday? (fly)
Because I had an interview for a job.

4 What .... he .... ? (do)
He's writing a letter.

5 When .... she .... her job? (lose)
About six weeks ago.

6 When .... he .... those clients in Cairo? (meet)
Next week.

7 What .... you .... if you lose your job? (do)
I'll probably start my own business.

8 What time .... the office .... ? (close)
At 5.30 p.m., usually.

9 How long .... you .... here? (work)
I've been with this company since 1978.

C PRACTICE

A reporter for the *In Business* programme is interviewing an American manager, Bruce Kulp, about his career and his recent experience of unemployment. Before the reporter begins the interview, she needs to check a few facts.

1 Here are the reporter's notes. What questions does she want to ask?

BRUCE KULP INTERVIEW - FACTS TO CHECK

LOOKING FOR WORK
1 How long/take/find another job?
2 How many jobs/apply for?

EARLY CAREER
3 What/first job?

LAST JOB
4 When/join/Exsel Incorporated?
5 What/you/do at Exsel?
6 Why/lose/job?

PRESENT JOB
7 How/hear about/Rochester Telephone?
8 What/you/do/Rochester Telephone?
9 How long/work there?
10 Like/new job?

2 Listen and compare your questions with the questions the reporter asks.

3 Now listen to the interview and write down Bruce Kulp's answers to the reporter's questions.

D

SPEAKING AND LISTENING

1 Here is some advice for someone who is unemployed and looking for work. With a partner, decide whether you think each point is good or bad advice.

a Take a holiday before you start looking for a new job.
b Looking for a job is the same as *doing* a job – you need to work full-time on it.
c Give yourself a little free time every week to relax.
d Exchange information and ideas with other unemployed people.
e Apply for as many jobs as possible – even jobs you don't really want.
f Talk to friends and other business contacts regularly – they are often the first to hear about a new job offer.

2 What other advice would you give to someone looking for work?

3 Now listen to the second part of the interview, where Bruce Kulp gives his own opinions. What does he think about points a-f above? Put a tick (✓) if Bruce agrees with the advice, and a cross (✗) if he disagrees.

E

PRONUNCIATION

Here are some long words.

information	responsible	competition
application	occasionally	regularly
experience	situation	incorporated
manufacturing	unemployment	immediately

1 How many syllables do they have? Where is the main stress? Put each of the words into one of these five groups. The first one is done for you.

a ■ - - -	
b - ■ - -	
c - - ■ -	*information*
d - - ■ - -	
e - ■ - - -	

2 Now listen and check your answers.

3 You will hear some phrases which include the words in the list. Listen and repeat.

12.2 In the office

Comparatives and superlatives (2)

more / the most   *less / the least*   *fewer / the fewest*

SEE LANGUAGE FILE: 6

A VOCABULARY AND SPEAKING

a

b

c

1 Look at the photos. Where would you prefer to work? Why?

2 The words on the right are the opposites of the words on the left, but the letters are scrambled. Unscramble the letters and match the opposites. The first one is done for you.

stressful	NEXARGIL *relaxing*	expensive	PHACE
noisy	TIQUE	sociable	BEALUSICON
boring	EGERINSTINT	good	DAB
efficient	FINEFINETIC	difficult	SAYE

Which of these adjectives would you use to describe the three office situations in **1**? Write some sentences with comparative or superlative forms of each adjective.

Working in an office is more expensive than working at home.
Working at home is the least stressful way of working.

3 Compare your answers with a partner and explain your reasons.

Working at home is cheaper because you don't have to pay for travel.

B

SPEAKING AND READING

1 The person working at home in photo b is a 'teleworker'. How many of these questions can you answer?

a What exactly is a 'teleworker'?
b What contact do teleworkers have with their office or head office?
c What percentage of people in your country work at home, do you think?
d Why is the number of teleworkers increasing?
e What are the disadvantages of teleworking?

2 Now read the text. What are the writer's answers to questions a-e above. Do they agree with your own answers?

TELEWORKING

The case for and against

Would you like to be a teleworker? Teleworkers are people who work *for* companies, but not *in* companies. That is to say, they do company work at home, usually on computers.

Teleworkers communicate with their supervisors by telephone or fax. They usually transfer information from their own computer to the office computer by electronic means. Some companies also give video phones to their home workers so they can see colleagues when they speak to them.

'Teleworking' is becoming more and more popular in Britain and in the USA; (in the USA, it is called 'telecommuting'). At the moment, about 6% of the working population employed by companies work at home, but experts estimate that this will rise to more than 15% before the end of the century.

There are many reasons for this increase. The biggest advantage for companies is that teleworking reduces their running costs. Fewer employees at work means less office space. Also, computers are now quicker and easier to use, and the price has fallen sharply. For a company which needs more manpower, one of the cheapest solutions can be to train employees in computer skills and to give them a personal computer to use at home.

But before you apply for a job as a teleworker, you should ask yourself if it is really the best situation for you. Bill Farrar, who works for a big paper recycling company, hasn't enjoyed his last three months at home. 'I often fall asleep at the computer because I don't have anybody to talk to,' he says. 'So, at lunchtimes, I often go to the nearest bar – which is just at the end of my road – and then the afternoon is gone!' Next week, he's starting a new job in a company where there are five people in one small office. 'I can't wait!' he says.

C

LANGUAGE FOCUS

1 Here are some expressions from the text in B. Write the opposite. One is done for you as an example.

a more and more popular
b the biggest
c quicker
d easier *more difficult/less easy*
e one of the cheapest solutions
f the best situation
g the nearest bar

2 *Fewer employees at work means less office space.*
Why do we say ***fewer*** *employees* but ***less*** *office space*?

LANGUAGE NOTE

Comparing quantity

In Unit 7.1 (page 89) we looked at ways of comparing adjectives.
This is how you compare quantity with countable [C] and uncountable [U] nouns.

1 Smaller quantity:

	comparative	superlative
[C]	*fewer*	*the fewest*
[U]	*less*	*the least*

Luxembourg has the fewest inhabitants [C] *of all the EC countries.*
Manual workers earn less money [U] *than managers.*

2 Bigger quantity:

	comparative	superlative
[C] + [U]	*more*	*the most*

The USA has more teleworkers [C] *than Britain.*
We gave him the job because he has the most experience [U].

D

PRACTICE

Complete each sentence with one of these words.

fewer	fewest	more
less	least	most

1 I always have a very quick lunch, so I have .... time to work in the afternoon.
2 We'll test all the computer programmes, and we'll buy the one that has the .... technical problems.

3 If .... people decide to work at home, we will spend .... money on office rent.
4 There are .... jobs in agriculture than there were fifty years ago.
5 Of all the countries in the world, Japan uses the .... robots for industrial production.
6 There were .... tourists than last year because of the bad weather.
7 I think I'll go by plane because it takes the .... time.

E

SPEAKING

1 Many people spend more time in their office than at home. How many things can you think of which can be used to decorate or personalize an office?

With a partner, continue the three lists below.

on your desk	on the walls	in the room
a photo of your wife/husband	certificates showing your qualifications	a drinks cabinet

2 Of course, your professional image is also important when you personalize your office. For example, a poster of a nude model behind your desk would probably not be suitable!

In your country, what kind of things present a good or a bad image? Think of offices you have visited.

12.3 Company culture

Past obligation

could couldn't didn't have to

SEE LANGUAGE FILE: 18

A

SPEAKING

1 What do you want from your job? Look at this list and add any other points you can think of.

- ☐ a good salary
- ☐ a job for life
- ☐ the chance to learn something new
- ☐ opportunities for promotion
- ☐ a good boss
- ☐ a good team of people to work with
- ☐ the chance to develop your own ideas
- ☐ ....
- ☐ ....

2 Now number them from 1 (most important) to 7, 8, or 9 (least important).

When you have finished, compare your answers with a partner.

B

READING

WPA is a successful insurance company in Britain. The Managing Director, Julian Stainton, has some interesting rules and regulations for his employees.

Read the list of company rules opposite and decide which of the five headings below matches the rules (1-5).

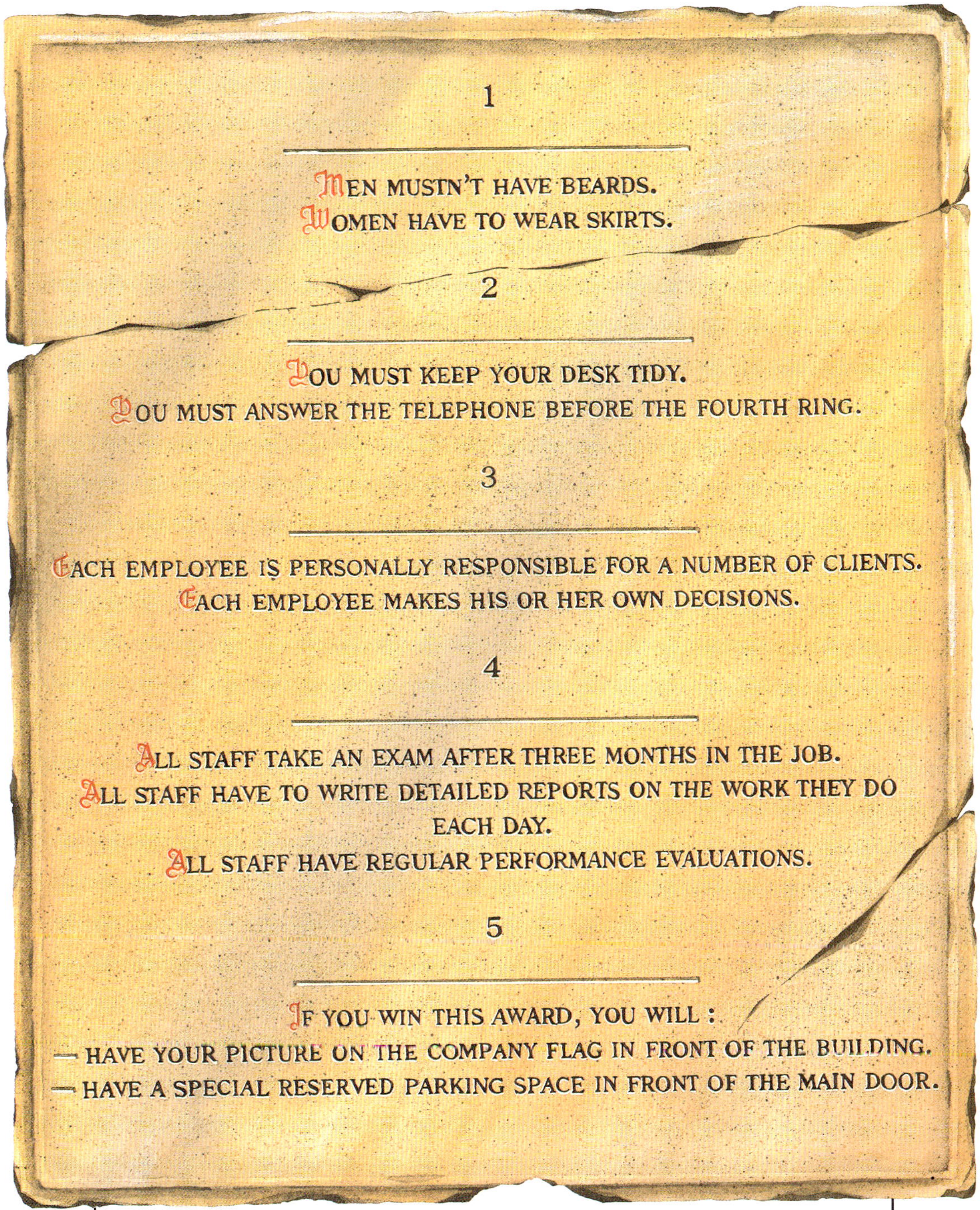

1

______

Men mustn't have beards.
Women have to wear skirts.

2

______

You must keep your desk tidy.
You must answer the telephone before the fourth ring.

3

______

Each employee is personally responsible for a number of clients.
Each employee makes his or her own decisions.

4

______

All staff take an exam after three months in the job.
All staff have to write detailed reports on the work they do each day.
All staff have regular performance evaluations.

5

______

If you win this award, you will:
— have your picture on the company flag in front of the building.
— have a special reserved parking space in front of the main door.

C

VOCABULARY

Find words and expressions in the text above (including the headings) that mean:

1 the way you look
2 systems at work
3 in good order/well organized
4 an interview to talk about your progress
5 a special prize
6 a place to put your car

D

SPEAKING

1 Which rules at WPA do you agree or disagree with? Why do you think the Managing Director has created these rules? Do you have anything like the 'Employee of the Month' award in your company?

2 Imagine that you are the Managing Director of a company (maybe your present company). What rules would you introduce immediately?

LANGUAGE NOTE

Past obligation

In Unit 10.2 (page 127) we looked at ways of describing present job responsibilities using *can, must, have to, mustn't, can't,* and *don't have to.*

This is how we talk about responsibilities in the past. Note that *must* and *mustn't* have no past tense form – instead, we use *had to* and *couldn't.*

	Present	Past
Permitted	*I can do it.*	*I could do it.*
Necessary	*I must/have to do it.*	*I had to do it.*
Not permitted	*I mustn't/can't do it.*	*I couldn't do it.*
Not necessary	*I don't have to do it.*	*I didn't have to do it.*

E

LISTENING AND SPEAKING

Jean-Pierre Poquet and Mercedes Villez were asked to talk about the worst job they have ever had.

1 Listen. What job did each of them do?

2 Listen again and make four sentences for each person.

Jean-Pierre Poquet	*didn't have to* *had to* *had to* *couldn't*	*phone people at home.* *keep people talking for five minutes.* *accept 'no' as an answer.* *visit the clients himself.*
Mercedes Villez	*had to* *didn't have to* *couldn't* *could*	*visit London in the morning.* *use a particular book in class.* *prepare lessons.* *change the style of the lessons.*

3 What's the worst job you've ever had? (Perhaps it was your first job, or a job you did when you were a student.) Tell a partner about your job, using *could, couldn't, had to,* and *didn't have to.*

Information Gap Files

FILE A
Unit 1.2
(PAGE 15)

PERSON A:

1 You work for the company below. Answer your partner's questions.

The company is Nintendo. It is based in Kyoto, 320 miles south of Tokyo. The company designs and manufactures computer games for children. It has a full-time staff of about 3,000. It has an annual turnover of more than $4 billion.

2 Person B works for a big company. Ask them questions to get more information. Complete the table below.

Company	
Activity	
Location	
Turnover	
Sales	

FILE B
Unit 1.4
(PAGE 23)

PERSON A:

You are the receptionist at the Belmondo Tennis Club. Give Person B the information he or she asks for:

Distance: *5 km from the town centre*
Time needed to get there: *20 minutes by car, 30 minutes by bus*
Membership: *£150 per year or £15 per month*
Cost per game: *the first 10 hours per month are free, then £3 per hour*
Other facilities: *bar and restaurant*
Number of members: *170*

FILE C
Unit 2.2
(PAGE 31)

PERSON A:

You are the receptionist at The Plaza Hotel, New York.
Note the name of the caller (Person B) and the reservation dates.

Prices: Single $250; Double $315

Ask caller to confirm booking by fax. Your fax number is: 212-759 3167.

FILE D
Unit 2.3
(PAGE 34)

PERSON A:

You are the travel agent. Isabelle Dussart comes to see you. Look at the information below and answer her questions.

	London (Heathrow)	New York* (JFK)
BA 117	08.45	12.05
BA 175	11.00	14.05
BA 177	13.45	16.35
BA 179	18.30	21.35

* NEW YORK TIME = LONDON TIME MINUS 5 HOURS
STANDARD SINGLE FARE: £422 + TAX (APPROXIMATELY £15)

FILE E
Unit 2.3
(PAGE 35)

PERSON B:

Listen to Person A. When you hear one of your times, circle it on your card. When you have circled all the times on your card, you have won. Shout 'Bingo!'.

09·25	03·40	14·15
02·00	12·30	06·05
15·10	11·45	23·35

FILE F
Unit 3.1
(PAGE 38)

PERSON A:

You are checking in to the Randolph. Answer the receptionist's questions using the information below.

You have a reservation.
Your name is Otto Weiss.
You want to stay for five nights.
You work for AEK in Vienna.
You are Austrian.
You want to pay with American Express.
You want a call at 6.30 a.m.

FILE G
Unit 3.3
(PAGE 43)

PERSON A:

You are the receptionist at The Randolph Hotel in Oxford. Person B wants to go to London this evening to see the musical *Sunset Boulevard*. Answer his/her questions using the information below.

OXFORD TO LONDON (PADDINGTON)

Oxford	Didcot	Reading	London
17.25	–	–	18.10
17.55	18.30	–	19.05

OXFORD NIGHTCABS
Need a taxi between 11 p.m. and 8 a.m.?
Call us
on (08165) 56431

LONDON (PADDINGTON) TO OXFORD

London	Reading	Didcot	Oxford
22.35	–	–	23.20
23.25	00.05	00.25	01.05

SUNSET BOULEVARD
The new musical by Andrew Lloyd Webber
ADELPHI THEATRE
(15 mins taxi from Paddington Station)
Performance 7.45 p.m. *(finishes 10.45 p.m.)*

FILE H
Unit 3.3
(PAGE 44)

PERSON A:

1 Look at your map. You are at Charing Cross Station. Person B asks you for help. Give him/her directions. The Prince of Wales Theatre is number 6.

2 Now choose another place on the map. Ask Person B for directions.

FILE I
Unit 6.3
(PAGE 35)

PERSON C:

Listen to Person A. When you hear one of your times, circle it on your card. When you have circled all the times on your card, you have won. Shout 'Bingo!'.

18·45	05·05	16·10
20·00	10·55	11·15
22·20	09·40	07·30

FILE J
Unit 6.2
(PAGE 80)

PERSON A:

Prepare the questions you need to ask to complete your table. Then ask Person B the questions.

When is Mrs Moinard arriving?

Name	Nationality	Arriving at:	Date	Time
	Japanese			22.10
Mr Mason		Heathrow Airport		
Mr Jacobsen	Danish		13 June	13.27
Mrs Moinard	French			11.12
Mr Gardini	Italian	Heathrow Airport	13 June	16.15
Mr Haffner	German	Gatwick Airport	13 June	08.55
Mrs Lacunza	Spanish	Gatwick Airport	14 June	05.45

FILE K
Unit 10.3
(PAGE 131)

PERSON A:

There are two different situations.

1 You are the manager of the Plaza Hotel in Brighton. Your receptionist took a reservation by phone last week. Unfortunately she didn't write the details very clearly, and she's on holiday this week. Phone Mr Brearly (Person B) and check all the details. Don't forget to say sorry if there's a mistake.

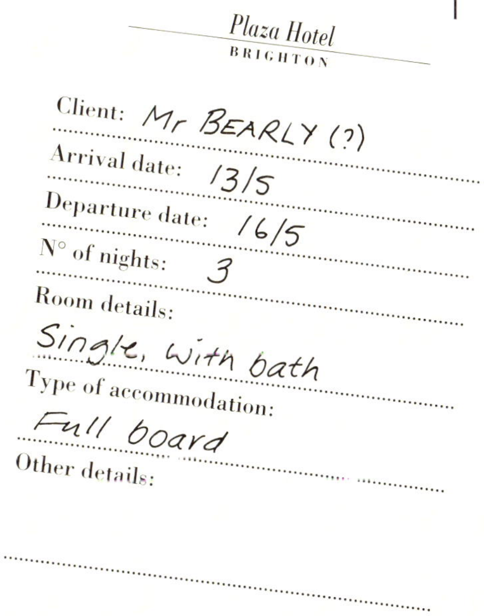
Plaza Hotel
BRIGHTON

Client: Mr BEARLY (?)
Arrival date: 13/5
Departure date: 16/5
N° of nights: 3
Room details:
Single, with bath
Type of accommodation:
Full board
Other details:

2 You are Mr(s) Dobson of Artlife Creations. Yesterday you received some goods from ASTA Plastics, but the contents didn't correspond to what you ordered. This morning you faxed ASTA Plastics to tell them there was a problem. Someone from ASTA (Person B) will phone you to check the details of the order.

This is what you wanted:
– 150 green picture frames, code 146/97
– 250 blue picture frames, code 146/58
– 500 plastic covers, code 574/99
– 250 plastic tubes (80 cm long), code 564/43

FILE L
Unit 9.4
(PAGE 120)

PERSON A:

There are two different situations.

1 You are Hans Steffenberg, Chief Accountant of FKT. You received an invoice from SIMCO for £6,000. You are sure this is too high.

- a Phone SIMCO and ask to speak to Mr Bush, Accounts Manager. Explain the problem and ask him to look into it. The invoice number is 6748, dated 23rd February.
- b Mr Bush phones you back.

2 You are Mr Geraldo, Production Manager of Valio Inc.

- a You receive a call from Simon Richards. He has a problem with an order of glasses you sent him last week. Say you'll look into the problem and that you'll call him back.
- b Call him back. Say sorry – order sent to wrong address – order returned to factory this morning. Ask for correct address. Promise to send glasses today.

FILE M
Unit 7.2
(PAGE 94)

Here are the correct answers.

a General Motors
b USA
c USA (Sears Tower, Chicago)
d China
e Amazon
f France (TGV)
g Japan (Seto-Ohashi bridge)
h Roosevelt

FILE N
Unit 7.3
(PAGE 97)

Here are the correct answers.

1	Walkman	1978
2	Scotch transparent tape	1925
3	Tabasco sauce	1868
4	Apple Macintosh	1984
5	Ray Ban sunglasses	1930
6	Monopoly	1935
7	Swatch	1983
8	Post-It	1974
9	Austin Mini	1959
10	Levis 501	1890
11	Jumbo Jet	1969
12	Polaroid Camera	1948

FILE O
Unit 2.3
(PAGE 35)

PERSON D:

Listen to Person A. When you hear one of your times, circle it on your card. When you have circled all the times on your card, you have won. Shout 'Bingo!'.

17·50	07·20	04·55
19·10	08·45	13·05
21·30	12·15	10·00

FILE P
Unit 11.2
(PAGE 139)

PERSON A:

Look at Luis Antonio de Oliveira's CV. Some of the information is missing. Ask Student B for the missing information.

Where was he born?

Name	Luis Antonio DE OLIVEIRA
Date of Birth	25.1.56
Place of Birth	........................, Brazil
Nationality	Brazilian
Address	53, rua Maria Angelica .... Rio de Janeiro, Brazil
Phone	(55) 21.227.17.98
Marital Status	Married, two children (aged 4 and 2). Married 19......

EMPLOYMENT HISTORY

1992-present	**Medilab, Rio de Janeiro.** Responsible for Clinical Trials (Antibiotics)
19......-92	**Merck, Buenos Aires.** Assistant Marketing Manager.
1988-90	**Schering Plough,** .... USA Product Manager.
1982-86	**Médecins Sans Frontières, Peru.** Project Manager, Vaccination Programs.

EDUCATION

1986-88	U.C.L.A., Los Angeles, USA. Masters in Business Administration. (Major: ....)
1975-82	Medical School. Graduated 1982 *cum laude.*
1970-......	Vasco da Gama High School, São Paulo

INTERESTS

astronomy, entomology, hang-gliding, football.

Clean Driving Licence

Language File

1 Cardinal and ordinal numbers

SEE 1.3 6.2

Cardinal		Ordinal (e.g. for dates)	
1	one	1st	first
2	two	2nd	second
3	three	3rd	third
4	four	4th	fourth
5	five	5th	fifth
6	six	6th	sixth
7	seven	7th	seventh
8	eight	8th	eighth
9	nine	9th	ninth
10	ten	10th	tenth
11	eleven	11th	eleventh
12	twelve	12th	twelfth
13	thirteen	13th	thirteenth
14	fourteen	14th	fourteenth
15	fifteen	15th	fifteenth
16	sixteen	16th	sixteenth
17	seventeen	17th	seventeenth
18	eighteen	18th	eighteenth
19	nineteen	19th	nineteenth
20	twenty	20th	twentieth
21	twenty-one	21st	twenty-first
22	twenty-two	22nd	twenty-second
30	thirty	30th	thirtieth
31	thirty-one	31st	thirty-first
40	forty	40th	fortieth
50	fifty	50th	fiftieth
60	sixty	60th	sixtieth
70	seventy	70th	seventieth
80	eighty	80th	eightieth
90	ninety	90th	ninetieth
100	a hundred	100th	hundredth
110	a hundred and ten		

1,000 a thousand

5,342 five thousand three hundred and forty-two

100,000 a hundred thousand

1,000,000 (1m) a million

2 Countries and nationalities

SEE 1.1

Nationalities with *-ish*

Country	Nationality
Britain	British
England	English
Scotland	Scottish
Ireland	Irish
Sweden	Swedish
Poland	Polish
Denmark	Danish
Spain	Spanish
Turkey	Turkish

Nationalities with *-an*

Country	Nationality
Italy	Italian
Russia	Russian
Hungary	Hungarian
Korea	Korean
Brazil	Brazilian
America	American
Germany	German
Belgium	Belgian
Mexico	Mexican

Nationalities with *-ese*

Country	Nationality
China	Chinese
Portugal	Portuguese
Japan	Japanese

Others

Country	Nationality
France	French
Holland	Dutch
Switzerland	Swiss

3 Time and date expressions

SEE 4.1, 6.1, 6.2, 8.1, 11.2

1 Describing a point in time

On *Sunday, Monday...*
Sunday morning, Tuesday afternoon, Monday evening...

In *the morning/the afternoon/the evening*
January, February...
1970, 1985...

At *3 o'clock, half past five...*
Easter/Christmas
night

Ø *next Tuesday, next year...*
last month, last week...
every day, every year...

2 Describing duration

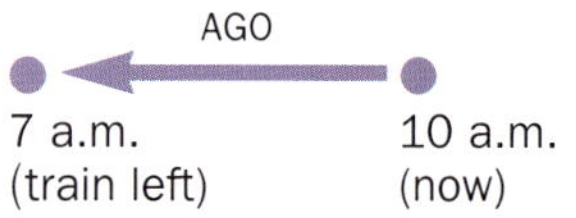

The train left three hours ago.

FROM 3 p.m.	FOR →	TO/UNTIL 5 p.m	*We spoke **from** 3 **to/until** 5 p.m.* *We spoke **for** two hours.*
SINCE Sunday	FOR →	Tuesday (today)	*I've been here **since*** Sunday.* ***for** two days.*

* *Since* is only used with the Present Perfect when the action started in the past and is continuing now.

3 The date relative to today

–3	three days ago
–2	the day before yesterday
–1	yesterday
0	TODAY
+1	tomorrow
+2	the day after tomorrow
+3	in three days (in three days' time)

4 Countable and uncountable nouns

SEE 3.1, 5.2

1 Nouns can be countable (C) or uncountable (U).

An uncountable noun:

a has no plural form
a lot of information (not ~~*informations*~~)

b cannot take the indefinite article *a/an*; we use *some* or Ø.
I'd like (some) information (not ~~*an information*~~)

2 When we express quantity, the words we use are sometimes different for countable and uncountable nouns.

(C)	(U)
Are there any faxes from Tokyo?	*Is there any news from Tokyo?*
How many weeks do we have?	*How much time do we have?*
I don't have many suitcases.	*I don't have much luggage.*
He gave me a few ideas.*	*He gave me a little* advice.*
We have very few rainy days.*	*We have very little* rain.*
He has fewer qualifications than me.	*He has less experience than me.*

* *A few / a little* is similar in meaning to *some*.
Few / little (no article) means *not many / not much*.

5 Personal pronouns and adjectives

A Subject pronouns — *I live in Paris. **She** works here.*
B Object pronouns — *I see **him** every week. Give it to **her**.*
C Possessive adjectives — *It's **my** book. It's **their** idea.*
D Possessive pronouns — *Whose car is that? It's **mine**.*

A	B	C	D
I	me	my	mine
you	you	your	yours
he	him	his	his
she	her	her	hers
we	us	our	ours
they	them	their	theirs

6 Making comparisons

SEE 7.1, 12.2

1 Comparison of adjectives

Adjective category	Adjective	Comparative	Superlative
One syllable	*old*	*older*	***the** oldest*
Ending in -*y*	*easy*	*easier*	***the** easiest*
Two syllables or more	*expensive*	***more** expensive* ***less** expensive*	***the most** expensive* ***the least** expensive*
Irregular forms	*good* *bad* *far*	*better* *worse* *further*	*the best* *the worst* *the furthest*

2 Comparing two things

*The ferry is cheaper **than** the plane* = *The ferry isn't **as** expensive **as** the plane.*

3 Intensifiers

The Channel Tunnel is	***much*** ***a lot*** ***slightly*** ***a little***	*cheaper* *more dangerous*	*than the plane.*

7 Letter-writing expressions

SEE 4.1, 9.1, 9.4, 11.3

We use different expressions for **formal** letters (e.g. to companies or to people we haven't met) and **informal** letters (e.g. to friends or to people we know well).

	Formal	**Informal**
Opening	*Dear Sir/Madam* *Dear Mr Jones* *Dear Sirs (Brit.)* *Gentlemen (Am.)*	*Dear Maria*
Saying thank you	*Thank you for...*	*Thanks for...*
Reason for writing	*I am writing to* *inform you that...* *enquire about...* *apologize for...*	*I am writing to* *tell you...* *ask you about...* *say sorry for...*
Asking for help	*Please could you... ?* *I would be grateful if you could... ?*	*Could you... ?* *Can you...*
Offering help	*We will be pleased/ happy to (send you)...*	*I'll (send you)...*
Enclosed documents	*I enclose...* *Please find enclosed (my CV)...*	*I'm sending you...*
Closing remark	*I look forward to* *hearing from you.* *meeting you* *seeing you.*	*(I'm) looking forward* *to hearing from you.* *to seeing you again.*
Finishing	*Yours faithfully* (Brit.)* *Yours sincerely** *Sincerely yours (Am.)* *Yours truly (Am.)*	*Best Wishes* *Best Regards* *Yours*

* In British English, *Yours faithfully* is used for letters which begin *Dear Sir/Dear Madam, Dear Sirs*. *Yours sincerely* is used when the letter begins *Dear Mr (Mrs) Jones*.

8 Telephone expressions

SEE 3.2, 6.3, 9.4

Finding your correspondent	*Can I/ I'd like to speak to Lisa, please.* *Can you put me through to Diana Carter?* *Hello, is that Mr. Mancini?*
Identifying yourself	*This is Tom Carter (speaking).* *Tom Carter here.*
Identifying the caller	*Who's calling/speaking please?* *Could you give me your name, please?* *Which company are you from?*
Asking caller to wait	*Hold on, please/Hold the line, please.* *I'm trying to connect you.* *Could you call back later?* *Can Mrs Carter call you back?*
Explaining absence	*I'm afraid/I'm sorry, but he's in a meeting/with a client/off sick/on holiday.*
Leaving a message	*Could you take a message?* *Could/Can I leave a message?*
Taking a message	*Can I take a message?* *Would you like to leave a message?* *I'll pass on the message.* *I'll give him/her the message.*
Dealing with problems	*I think you've got the wrong number.* *Could you speak up – it's a bad line.* *Could you speak more slowly, please?*

9 Social expressions

SEE 2.2, 4.2, 5.3

Prompts	**Responses**
I'm Mr ... How do you do?	*How do you do./Pleased to meet you.* *My name's...*
Please take a seat.	*Thank you.*
Would you like some coffee?	*Yes, please.* *No, thank you.*
How are you? *How are things going?* *How's business?*	*Fine, thank you.* *Very well.* *Not so bad, thank you.*

Prompts	Responses
I'm sorry I'm late. *I'm afraid I can't come.*	*That's OK.* *Never mind.* *It doesn't matter.*
Can I leave early? *May I smoke?*	*Yes, of course.* *Yes, sure.* *No, I'm afraid that's not possible.* (+ give reason)
Could you help me for a minute?	*Yes, of course.* *Yes, sure.* *No, I'm afraid I can't.* (+ give reason)
Thank you very much.	*Not at all.* *You're welcome.* *Don't mention it.*
Shall I come back later? *Would you like me to leave?*	*No, that's OK. It's not necessary.*

10 Talking about companies and jobs

SEE 1.1, 2.1

Questions	Answers
Who do you work for?	*I work for...*
What does your company do?	*It makes/sells/distributes...*
Where is the company based/ located?	*It's (based/located) in...*
How many employees are there?	*We employ about...* (number) *people.*
What's your annual turnover? *What are your annual sales?*	*About...* (number)
What's the structure of the company?	*It consists of/ is divided into* (number) *divisions or departments.*
Where do you work?	*I work in...* (town, country)
What do you do?	*I'm a...* (job)
Which department are you in?	*I work in the.... department.*
Who are you responsible to?	*I'm responsible to the...* (position of person above you)
How long have you worked there?	*I've worked there since/for...* *I joined the company in...*

11 Present Simple tense

SEE 1.1, 1.3

Use:

for talking about permanent or regular actions.

Form:

AFFIRMATIVE	
I You	work.
He She It	works.
We They	work.

NEGATIVE*		
I You	don't	work.
He She It	doesn't	
We They	don't	

QUESTION		
Do	I you	work?
Does	he she it	
Do	we they	

* In the negative form, we generally use the contraction (*I don't = I do not; he doesn't = he does not*) in both spoken and informal written English.

12 Present Continuous tense

SEE 5.1, 5.2, 6.1, 6.2

Use:

for talking about:

a actions happening now, at this moment
b present projects
c fixed plans and appointments in the future

Form:

AFFIRMATIVE*	
I'm You're	working.
He's She's It's	
We're They're	

NEGATIVE		
I'm	not	working.
You	aren't	
He She It	isn't	
We They	aren't	

QUESTION		
Am	I	working?
Are	you	
Is	he she it	
Are	we	
Are	they	

* In the affirmative form, we generally use the contraction (*I'm = I am; we're = we are,* etc.) in both spoken and informal written English.

13 Past Simple tense

SEE 4.1, 8.1

Use:

for talking about past actions which have no relation to now.

Form:

AFFIRMATIVE*	
I	
You	
He	worked.
She	
We	
They	

NEGATIVE	
I	
You	
He	didn't work.
She	
We	
They	

QUESTION		
	I	
	You	
Did	He	work?
	She	
	We	
	They	

* Regular verbs all finish in *-ed* in the affirmative Past Simple form. Many verbs are irregular – there is a list in File 15.

14 Present Perfect tense

SEE 11.2, 11.3

Use:

a (with *for* and *since*) for talking about actions which started in the past and are continuing now.

b for talking about experiences in your life where the time or date in the past is not specified.

Form:

use *have* with the past participle (there is a list in File 15).

AFFIRMATIVE*	
I've	
You've	
He's	
She's	gone.
It's	
We've	
They've	

NEGATIVE		
I You	haven't	
He She It	hasn't	gone.
We They	haven't	

QUESTION		
Have	I you	
Has	he she it	gone?
Have	we they	

* In the affirmative form, we generally use the contraction (*I've* = I *have*; *he's* = *he has; she's* = *she has* etc.) in both spoken and informal written English.

15 Irregular verbs

SEE 4.1, Language Files 13 and 14

stem	past tense	past participle
be	was /were	been
become	became	become
begin	began	begun
break	broke	broken
bring	brought	brought
build	built	built
buy	bought	bought
catch	caught	caught
choose	chose	chosen
come	came	come
cost	cost	cost
cut	cut	cut
deal	dealt	dealt
do	did	done
draw	drew	drawn
drink	drank	drunk
drive	drove	driven
eat	ate	eaten
fall	fell	fallen
feel	felt	felt
find	found	found
fly	flew	flown
forbid	forbade	forbidden
forget	forgot	forgotten
get	got	got (*Am.* gotten)
give	gave	given
go	went	gone
grow	grew	grown
have	had	had
hear	heard	heard
hide	hid	hidden
hit	hit	hit
hold	held	held
hurt	hurt	hurt
keep	kept	kept
know	knew	known
lay	laid	laid
lead	led	led
learn	learnt	learnt
leave	left	left
lend	lent	lent

stem	past tense	past participle
let	let	let
lie	lay	lain
lose	lost	lost
make	made	made
mean	meant	meant
meet	met	met
pay	paid	paid
quit	quit	quit
read	read	read
ride	rode	ridden
ring	rang	rung
rise	rose	risen
run	ran	run
say	said	said
see	saw	seen
sell	sold	sold
send	sent	sent
set	set	set
shake	shook	shaken
shoot	shot	shot
show	showed	shown
shut	shut	shut
sing	sang	sung
sit	sat	sat
sleep	slept	slept
speak	spoke	spoken
spend	spent	spent
spread	spread	spread
stand	stood	stood
steal	stole	stolen
stick	stuck	stuck
swim	swam	swum
take	took	taken
teach	taught	taught
tell	told	told
think	thought	thought
throw	threw	thrown
understand	understood	understood
wear	wore	worn
win	won	won
write	wrote	written

16 Future with *will*

SEE 9.1, 9.2, 9.3, 9.4

Use:

a for making predictions about the future
b for making decisions about the future

For talking about our fixed plans, don't use *will*, use the Present Continuous. (see File 12).

Form:

AFFIRMATIVE*		NEGATIVE*		QUESTION		
I'll You'll He'll She'll We'll They'll	work.	I You He She We They	won't work.	Will	I you he she we they	work?

* In the affirmative and negative form, we generally use the contraction (*I'll = I will; we'll = we will; he won't = he will not,* etc.) in both spoken and informal written English.

17 *Here* and *there*

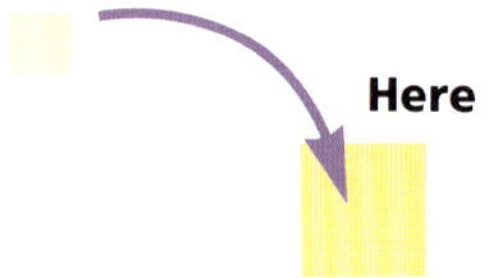

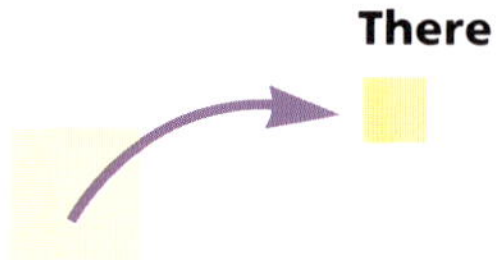

This *company is very big.* (= my company)	***That*** *company is much smaller.* (= another company)
I'm *working* ***this*** *week* (now)	*I'll be/I was in Paris* ***that*** *week.* (a week in the past or future)
These *books* (in my hand)	***Those*** *books* (on the other side of the room)
Come here! *A salesman* ***came*** *to our company.*	*Can you* ***go*** *to the post office?* *I often* ***go*** *to the USA on business.*
Can you ***bring*** *me the bill, please?* *When you* ***come*** *to visit us,* ***bring*** *your tennis racket.*	*Can you* ***take*** *this letter to Mr Simpson, please?* *I was late for my flight, so he* ***took*** *me to the station in his car.*
He ***lent*** *me $50.*	*He* ***borrowed*** *$50 from me.*

18 Modal verbs

SEE 2.2, 9.2, 10.1, 10.2, 10.3, 12.3

Verb	Use/Meaning	Example
have to/ must	obligation/necessity	*I **have to** work five days a week.* *I **must** leave at 4 o'clock to catch my train.*
mustn't	not permitted	*I **mustn't** smoke here – it's a non-smoking office.*
don't have to	not necessary	*I **don't have to** work on Sundays.*
can (can't)	possibility ability permission request (informal)	*I **can** meet you next week.* *I **can't** swim.* ***Can** I leave early?* ***Can** you help me, please?*
may	permission	***May** I smoke?*
could (couldn't)	request permitted (in the past)	***Could** you tell me the address?* *In my first job, I **couldn't** leave the office early.*
should (shouldn't)	recommending / advising	*I think we **should** accept the proposal.* *You **shouldn't** do that, it's not a good idea.*
shall	suggesting offering	***Shall** we finish now and go for coffee?* ***Shall** I bring you the bill now, sir?*
would	offering	***Would** you like a coffee?* ***Would** you like to eat?* ***Would** you like me to help you?*

Modal verbs in the past (see page 154)

Present	Past
I can do it.	*I **could** do it.*
I must do it. *I have to do it.*	*I **had to** do it.*
I mustn't do it. *I can't do it.*	*I **couldn't** do it.*
I don't have to do it.	*I **didn't have to** do it.*

19 Prepositions of place

SEE 3.3

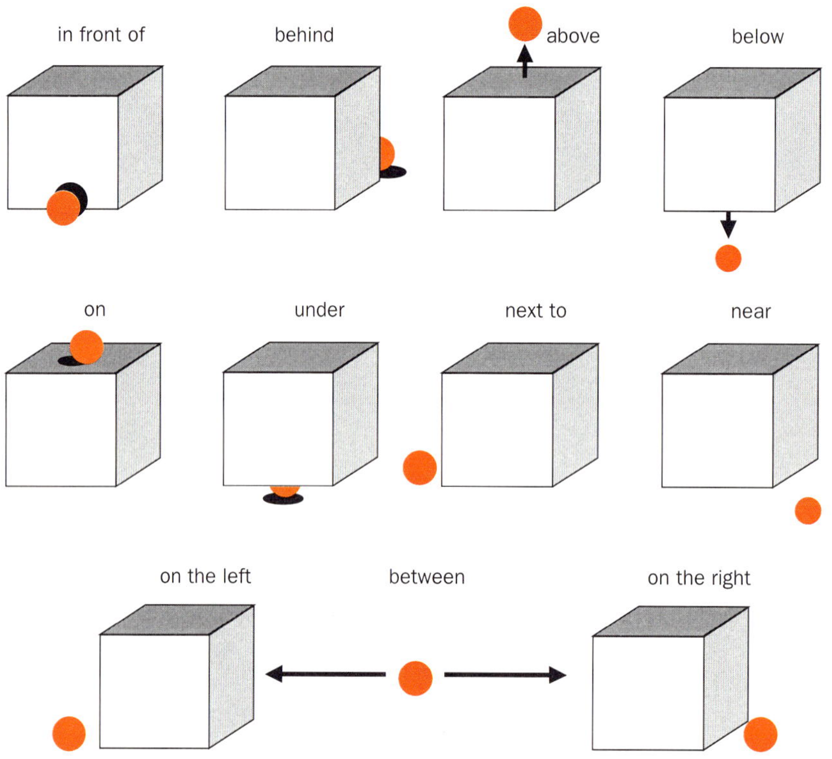

20 Prepositions of movement

SEE 3.3

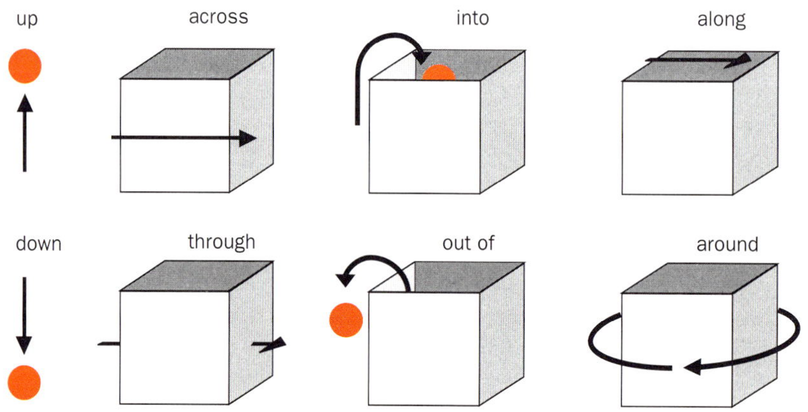

Preposition of movement are normally used with verbs of movement.
He walked ***along*** *the corridor. He came* ***into*** *the room.*

Sometimes the verb is not a verb of movement.
He showed me ***around*** *the factory.* *He looked* ***out of*** *the window.*

Tapescript

1

You and your company

1.1 People in business

A

A Just a few questions Mr Olofson. It won't take long.
B That's fine.
A Who do you work for exactly? I understand it's a division of Sony.
B Yes, the full name is Sony Electronic Publishing.
A Sony... Electronic... Publishing... . And you're the President of the company. Excuse me, but you're very young.
B Yes...well...it's a very young company.
A And where do you live and work?
B In the United States.
A But you are from Iceland?
B Yes, that's right.
A And what does your company do? Do you make hi-fis? TVs?
B No, we make video games and software.
A Video games? Do you play them at home?
B No, I don't take my work home. When I'm at home, I write. That takes a lot of my time.
A That's interesting. What sort of things do you write?
B Novels and short stories, mainly.
A Is this one of your books?
B Yes, it is.
A Absolution.. Oh, your name's Olafsson. Let me change that in my notebook. O-L-A-F-double S-O-N. But there's one thing I don't understand. You run a big division of an international company and you write novels? How do you find the time?
B Well, I travel a lot, so I have free time to work in the evenings, in my hotel room. And at weekends, of course.

E

A Hello, is that Sally?
B Yes, hello, Miguel. Where are you?
A I'm in Paris. I have an interview with Agnès B.
B Sorry. Who?
A Agnès B. She's a clothes designer.
B Listen – this is a bad line. Can you say that again?
A Agnes , that's A-G-N-E-S, then B, the letter B.
B What's the name of her company?
A It's the same name, Agnès B – you know, the fashion boutique.
B Ah yes, of course. And she's French, I suppose.
A Yes, that's right.
B OK, but have you got anybody else from Europe?
A Yes, I have an interview with Alan Yentob.
B Can you spell that?
A Yes. Y-E-N-T-O-B.
B Where's he from?
A He's from England. He's the Controller of BBC 1, the television station.
B OK, not bad. Anybody else?
A No, that's all for the moment.
B Well. Alan Yentob and Agnès B are both European. How about someone from outside Europe? Maybe the Far East? South America? We need to be more international.
A Yes, I agree. I'm looking. I'll call you back tomorrow.

F

Spanish	Britain
Portugal	Sweden
Portuguese	Canada
Italian	Canadian
Italy	Netherlands
Japan	Norwegian
Japanese	
Germany	
German	

1.2 Talking about your company

A

Hi. Here at Starbucks we manufacture coffee. Not just any coffee; we specialize in high-quality coffee, and we go all over the world to buy it. We sell the coffee in stores in the US and Canada – about 400 stores. Many of our stores are located on the West Coast, but we now also have stores in Washington DC, on the East Coast. Our company is based in Seattle – that's where the head office is, and that's where our first stores were.

Americans drink a lot of coffee. They are interested in quality, and that's why they drink our coffee. Our sales for this year are $285 million, and we have an annual growth rate of more than 75%.

The President of our company is Howard Schultz. Starbucks employs 6,000 people, 60% of them part-time. All 6,000 employees are shareholders in the company. That probably surprises you. You see, Mr Schultz's philosophy is this: the customer and the employee both come first. If our people are happy, they make the customers happy.

1.3 Company facts and figures

F 1

a My company has nine factories in Europe.
b My daughter is thirteen this month.
c The train leaves from platform sixteen.
d There are eighty products in our catalogue.
e We employ ninety people in our New York office.

1.4 Work and leisure

A 3

1 Alan Yentob
A Do you have any free time in the morning before work?
B Yes, I often wake up early in the morning and I watch last night's programmes. I have a portable video near my bed, with headphones so I can listen without waking up the others. Sometimes I go to the swimming pool with my son, Jacob – he's a great swimmer.
A Do you do any other sports?
B I play tennis sometimes. But I don't do much sport, in general.
A What about lunch? Is it a time to relax? Or do you work through lunch?
B Well, I have to see a lot of people, as you can imagine, so lunch is often just a sandwich in my office during a meeting. But on the way to work there's a small hotel, and I sometimes have breakfast meetings there in the morning. I enjoy my food, but during the day it's not really relaxation.
A And in the evening?
B I try to be home before eight o'clock, when Jacob goes to bed. Sometimes Philippa and I cook dinner at home for friends. I enjoy cooking, like a lot of men. Now for me, that is relaxing.

2 Agnès B
A How do you spend your morning?
B Well, my day begins with breakfast: coffee and a little bread and butter, and I think about my day. I don't talk, and I don't read the newspaper. Then I cycle

to work.
A You go to work by bicycle?
B Yes, it's very relaxing. It takes me about 15 minutes. I usually arrive at our new office on the rue Dieu at about half past ten.
A Do you get time to relax during the day? To go out for a meal, for example?
B Not always, no. When we are very busy we eat in the office. And when we prepare the new collections, for example, we have dinner at work every night. A cook comes and prepares the food.
A Do you go out to the shops to see your competitors' designs?
B No, I don't. Maybe that's surprising, but I never go into a clothes shop, never. I follow my own ideas. When I'm at home, I sometimes try clothes on in front of the mirror, and that helps me a lot in my work.
A And what about your evenings?
B Well, when we are not too busy, I usually leave the office at about 7. I love going out in the evening.
A Where do you go?
B To jazz or rock concerts, or to dinner with friends. I never go to bed before one or two in the morning.

2

Preparing a trip

2.1 Choosing a hotel

B

A Larry, could you tell me a little about New York?
B Sure. What would you like to know?
A Is it expensive?
B It depends. What is your budget?
A $250 a day. How much is a hotel room?
B Between $150 and $300. How many days are you staying there?
A Three.
B Where are you working?
A At the Rockefeller Center – 5th Avenue and 51st Street. Are there any hotels in that part of town?
B Of course. But Rockefeller Center is a business centre. It's not very interesting at night. What do you want to do in the evenings?
A Go to a restaurant, go swimming, or maybe go to the ballet.
B There are some great restaurants in New York and there is usually a ballet at Lincoln Center. Choose a hotel in that area.
A Where's that?
B Midtown. Just off Central Park.
A That's dangerous, isn't it?
B Not at all. During the day it is full of people having lunch, jogging, horseback riding. It's a great place.
A Where can I find a list of hotels? Is there a guide?
B There are several. I'll lend you one.
A What about getting around?
B Don't use the subway. It's not very safe or clean. There are lots of yellow cabs. They are not very expensive.
A Thanks for your help.
B It's a pleasure.

2.2 Booking a hotel

A

A Good morning, Radisson Empire. Can I help you?
B Yes, I'd like to book a room, please.
A When exactly?
B Next month. For three nights. I arrive on the 8th of March and leave on the 11th of March .
A Hold the line, I'll check. Now then... single or double?
B Single, please.
A Arrival March 8th; departure March 11th. Yes, we have a single with bath.
B How much is it?
A $165 including breakfast plus tax.
B That's fine. Is there a swimming pool?
A Yes, there is. It's indoors.
B And how far is it to the Lincoln Center?
A It's just across the street.
B OK, I'll take it.
A Could I have your name, please?
B Dussart. Isabelle Dussart.
A Could you spell that, please?
B D-U-S-S-A-R-T.
A OK, Mrs Dussart. That's a single room with bath from March 8th to March 11th. Could you send us a fax to confirm your booking?
B Of course. Can you give me your fax number?
A Yes, it's 212 315 0349.
B Thank you for your help.
A Thank you for calling. Have a nice day.

2.3 Flying out

E

1
Y British Airways flight 651 for Athens leaves from Gate 17 at thirteen-fifty. Will passengers with tickets please proceed to gate 17 immediately. That's gate 17 for BA Flight 651 to Athens, departing at thirteen-fifty.

2
A Can you tell me the gate for the flight to New York at 12.30?
B Do you have the flight number?
A Yes, it's AA 215.
B AA 215. One moment. Yes, it's Gate 51.
A Thank you.

3
Y Passengers for SK Flight 444 to Stockholm are requested to board at Gate 14. That's Gate 14 for Flight SK 444. Departure time will be 14.05.

4
A Are there any seats on the next flight to Madrid?
B To Madrid? That's IB 414. Yes, there are. But you'll have to hurry.
A What time does it leave?
B Ten past two.
A Ten past two! Can you reserve me a seat?
B Yes, of course. Business or economy class?
A Business.

5
Y We regret to inform passengers on the fourteen-thirty flight to Tokyo that their departure has been delayed. That's a delay on Flight JL 519 to Tokyo, scheduled to depart at fourteen-thirty.

6
A Excuse me. Is the flight to Paris boarding now?
B Sorry, Madam. Which flight to Paris?
A The Air France flight.
B AF 661. Yes, it's boarding now at Gate 16. It's leaving at fifteen hundred.
A Pardon me. What time?
B At three o'clock.
A That's two hours late.
B Yes, I'm sorry about that, Madam.

3

Away on business

3.1 Arriving

A

Dialogue 1
A Good afternoon, sir. Could I see your passport, please.
B Certainly.
A Thank you. Are you here on business?
B Yes, I am.
A How many days are you staying?
B Three days.
A Enjoy your stay.
B Thank you very much.

Dialogue 2
A Could you open this bag, sir?
B Yes, of course.
A How many bags do you have?
B Just this one.
A Thank you very much.

Dialogue 3
A Can I help you?
B Yes. Could I cash a traveller's cheque, please?
A Yes, sir. Could you sign it at the bottom, please?

B There you are.
A Have you got any identification?
B My passport?
A Fine. OK, that's twenty, forty, sixty, eighty, a hundred pounds.

Dialogue 4

A Here you are, sir. The Randolph.
B Thanks. How much is that?
A Well, it's four pounds plus fifty pence for the bag. So that's four pounds fifty.
B Take five pounds. Have you got change for a twenty-pound note?
A Yes, of course. So that's fifteen pounds change – five, ten, fifteen.
B Thanks. Could I have a receipt, please?
A Certainly.

D

A Good evening, sir.
B Good evening. I have a reservation.
A Could I have your name please?
B Dillon. Robert Dillon.
A And your nationality?
B American.
A How many nights are you staying?
B Three.
A Who do you work for?
B KPMG.
A Have you got a car?
B No, I came by train.
A How would you like to pay?
B Visa, if that's OK.
A That's fine. Have you got any luggage?
B Just one bag.
A Would you like a morning call, Mr Dillon?
B Yes. Seven-thirty, please.
A OK. Your room number is 243. It's on the second floor. When you come out of the lift, turn left, and it is at the end of the corridor on the right. Enjoy your stay.

3.2 Going out

A

A Hello. Charles Mant's office.
B Hello. Could I speak to Mr Mant, please?
A I'm sorry, he's out. Can I take a message?
B Yes. Could you tell him Mr Dillon from KPMG called?
A Could I have your number, please?
B It's an Oxford number. My hotel number is 01865 247481. Can he call me back today?
A Yes. He'll be back soon. I'll ask him to call you.
B Thank you for your help.
A Thank you. Bye.

D

A The Randolph. Can I help you?
B Yes. Could I speak to Mr Dillon, please?
A Hold the line. I'll put you through to his room.
C Hello?
B Is that you, Robert?
C Speaking. Hello, Charles. Thanks for calling me back.
B How are you?
C Fine, and you?
B Very well. How long are you in England for?
C Just three days. Shall we meet one evening?
B Sure. When are you free?
C Tonight? What shall we do?
B Would you like to go to the theatre?
C I'd love to. What's on?
B Sunset Boulevard.
C That sounds great. What time does it start?
B Erm... 7.45.
C Where can we meet?
B Let's meet at a restaurant near the theatre. Call me back when you know the train times.
C OK. Speak to you later.
B Bye.

3.3 Arranging to meet

C

A Hello, Charles, it's me again.
B Hi, Robert. So, what time do you arrive?
A Er... ten past six at Paddington.
B OK, and the play starts at 7.45. Let's meet at the Café Fish at quarter to seven.
A Fine. How do I get there?
B Right. Take the underground to Leicester Square.
A Pardon me?
B Leicester Square. L-E-I-C-E-S-T-E-R Square.
A OK, right.
B Come out of the underground station and turn right. Go down Charing Cross Road past Wyndham's Theatre.
A OK.
B When you get to Irving Street, turn right and go as far as Leicester Square.
A Sorry, did you say Irvine Street?
B No, Irving Street. Leicester Square is at the end of Irving Street. There are always lots of people in Leicester Square — it's where all the big London cinemas are.
A Right.
B So go across Leicester Square and take the first street on the left. The restaurant is on the left opposite a flower shop.
A Thank you very much. See you there at 6.45.

3.4 Eating out

B

A I'm sure Sally will be here in a minute. There she is. Sally, this is an old friend of mine, Robert Dillon. Robert, this is my wife, Sally.
B Pleased to meet you, Sally.
C Nice to meet you, Robert. Have you ordered?
A No. We've just arrived.
D Are you ready to order?
A Yes, I think so. Sally. What would you like?
C Er... Cottage Pie, please.
B What exactly is that?
C It's minced meat cooked with mashed potato on top.
B Sounds nice, but I think I'll have the lasagne, please.
A And I'd like the Chilli, please.
D No starters?
A No, thanks, we're in a hurry.
D What would you like to drink?
C I'd like a glass of white wine, please.
A What would you like, Robert?
B I'd like red, please.
A Me too.
D So, that's one white wine and two glasses of red.
A Thanks very much.

E

A Well, that was very nice.
C Lovely.
B Can I pay?
A Not at all. You are my guest. This is on me. Excuse me?
D Yes?
A Can I have the bill, please? Do you take American Express?
D Yes, of course.
A And could I have a receipt, please?
D Certainly.
B Well thank you very much, Charles. That was excellent.

4
Visiting a company

4.2 Meeting new people

B

A Mr Kanemori, how do you do? I'm Mark Gordon, Personnel Officer. Welcome to ICL.
B Thank you.
A Did you have a good journey?
B Yes, thank you. It was a long flight, but I slept for a few hours.
A And are you happy with your hotel?
B Yes, it's very comfortable and it's in a good position.
A I'm pleased to hear that. Would you like a coffee before we start?
B No, thank you. I had a cup of coffee just now.
A So, is this your first visit to England?
B Yes, it is.
A Well, I hope you have a nice stay.
B Thank you very much. I'm sure I'll enjoy my visit here.

F

Hello. My name's Susanna.
Do you work for ICL?
Where are you from?
When did you arrive?
Did you have a good journey?
Is this your first visit to the company?
How's your hotel?
Would you like some coffee?
OK, I must go now. Have a nice day.

4.3 Explaining company structure

B

I'd just like to tell you something about how ICL is organized. As you know, we are now a subsidiary of Fujitsu, which is an 82% shareholder in our company. That, of course, is why you are here today, and we are very pleased to meet you all.

ICL employs a total of 24,000 people. Following our reorganization, the group now consists of 29 autonomous companies, each with its own Managing Director. ICL Group is divided into three operating divisions. The first is Industry Systems. This is the division which produces business solutions — software — for ICL's customers. The second is Technology, which manufactures computers and components. The third division is ICL Services, which sells computer services, like maintenance and training.

ICL was one of the first computer companies in the world to start producing different software products for specific markets. We now operate in six different target markets: firstly retail: that's shops, supermarkets and so on; then financial services; local and central government; healthcare; manufacturing; and finally, travel and transport.

Does anybody have any questions at this point?

E

production
produce
product
accounts
accountant
advertise
advertising
advertisement
purchase
purchasing
develop
development
recruit
recruitment
research

5 New developments

5.1 Current activities

C

A Linda Dawson.
B Hi, Linda. It's Michael.
A Michael! How's it going? Where are you?
B I'm in Sydney. I'm calling from the hotel.
A What time is it in Sydney?
B It's half past eight, in the evening. Actually, I'm having dinner right now. I'm calling from the restaurant.
A Is it urgent, Michael? I'm rather busy.
B No. Just a few questions. It can wait.
A Sorry, Michael. I'm getting ready for the sales meeting. What are you having?
B Having?
A For dinner. What are you eating?
B Oh! Lobster.
A Enjoy your lobster. Can I call you in a couple of hours?
B Sure. That's fine.
A Great. Bye.
B Bye.

F

1 Hello.
2 What time is it?
3 What are you doing?
4 What do you normally do at this time?
5 Do you smoke?
6 Do you like nice clothes?
7 What are you wearing?
8 Sounds nice!
9 What are you working on at the moment?
10 Sounds interesting.
11 Nice talking with you.

5.3 Personal developments

A

A Hello. I don't think we know each other.
B No, we don't. How do you do? I'm Bruno Retter.
A Pleased to meet you. My name's Jim Fenton.
B So, what do you do, Jim?
A I work for Global Systems. I'm a Sales Manager. Do you know us?
B Yes, I do. In fact, I think you did some work for us a few years ago. You see, I work in Research and Development at Simons International.
A Ah, yes. I remember the contract. So, who do you know here, Bruno?
B Just the host, and one or two others.
A Well, listen, let me introduce you to a few people. But I'll get you another drink first. What would you like?
B Thanks. Gin and tonic, please, with ice and lemon.

A Hello. Bruno Retter, isn't it?
B Jim. What a surprise to see you here! How are you?
A Not so bad. How's the job going at Simons?
B We're very busy. We're moving to new offices at the moment, because our branch is expanding. We're recruiting twenty new people.
A Well, I'm glad to hear that. You're doing very well then?
B Yes, we are. How about you? Are you still at Global Systems?
A Yes, I am – for the moment.
B And how are things going?
A Not very well, I'm afraid. We're losing a lot of orders – too much competition from the big operators.
B I'm sorry to hear that, Jim. I hope things get better soon. Anyway, is the family OK? How are Heidi and the children?
A Well, Heidi's still working at the hospital. Joe's studying for his exams at university and Hannah's still at school – she's visiting France with her class at the moment. They're all fine.
B That's good news. So, why are you here at Simons International?
A I'm looking for a new job. And I think Simons International wants to offer me one.
B Oh! That's ... great, Jim.

6 Arrangements

6.1 Future engagements

A

Part 1

A OK, so can we organize next week? You're going to Munich for the trade fair. When are you leaving, exactly?
B On Wednesday morning: the 8.30 plane from Heathrow, and I'm coming back the next day at about nine in the evening. The trade fair's on Wednesday afternoon and all day Thursday.
A You know that Paolo Lentini is coming on Thursday – I'm picking him up at the station at five.
B Yes, I know. But I think his train arrives at half past four, not five.
A Really? Let me check his fax. ... Yes, you're right. He's arriving at four-thirty. I must change that before I forget. ... Now, can we have a meeting with Paolo on Friday? You are working on Friday?
B Well, no, I'm not. I wanted to stay at home to write the report on my trip to Munich.
A I think Paolo really wants to see you, too. Can you come to the office?
B Well, OK. I can write my report at the weekend. So, that's a meeting with

Paolo Lentini all day Friday!
A Yes. Sorry about that!

Part 2
B What are *you* doing next week, Diana?
A I'm taking the train to Liverpool on Monday morning, and I'm visiting three clients in the afternoon. Then, on Wednesday, the Manager of OTC is coming – I'm showing him round the company. Oh, before I forget, we're having dinner with the sales team on Tuesday evening – I hope you're free.
B Yes, I am. I'm interviewing candidates for the marketing job all day Monday and Tuesday, but I'm free in the evening.
A OK, good.

6.2 Fixing the date

A

A November twenty-second, nineteen sixty-three
B The third of October, nineteen-ninety
C April eighteenth, nineteen oh six
D July twenty-first, nineteen sixty-nine

E

A So, the first person we have to meet is Mr Sato?
B Yes, he's arriving on the 10th June at Manchester airport.
A He's going to be quite late, is that right?
B Yes, that's right. His plane's landing at ten past ten in the evening. I'll send a taxi to meet him and take him to his hotel.

A Who's coming the next day?
B On the 11th we've got just one arrival at Heathrow Airport at 14.30, that's the American representative.
A Yes. Mr Mason, isn't it?

B OK. What about the 12th?
A Well, on the 12th we've got two people arriving at Victoria station. Mrs Moinard the French representative is arriving just after 11 o'clock. Then Mr Jacobsen's train comes in at 13.27.
B That's good. We can meet them at the same time.

A Who's coming on the 13th?
B Mr Gardini and Mr Haffner, both flying to London.
A Are they arriving at the same airport? Can we meet them together?
B I'm afraid not. Mr Gardini is landing at Heathrow and Mr Haffner at Gatwick.
A OK, so you can go and collect Mr Gardini. He's flying from Milan, arriving at 6.15.
B Sorry, six-fifteen, you said?
A Yes, that's right.

A When's the German representative coming?
B Mr Haffner? He's arriving on the 13th, too.
A What time's he arriving?
B At 8.55 in the morning, at Gatwick Airport.
A 8.55? I'll go and collect him.

A OK. Is that everybody?
B No. There's one late arrival - Mrs Lacunza. Her flight is on the 15th and she isn't arriving until quarter to six in the afternoon. I can meet her. ... And that's it.
A Great. I hope everybody arrives on time!

6.3 Getting connected

B

Conversation One
A Lakefield's. Good morning.
B Good morning. Can I speak to Mr Jones, please?
A Who's calling, please?
B This is Mr Pym of Technos.
A Can you spell your name, please?
B Certainly. That's P-Y-M.
A Hold the line please, Mr Pym. ... Hello, Mr Pym. I'm afraid he's in a meeting. Can I take a message?
B Yes. Could you tell him that I'd like to make an appointment for next week?
A Right, Mr Pym. I'll give him the message.

Conversation Two
A Lakefield's. Good morning.
B Hello. Can I speak to Mr Jones, please?
A Who's calling, please?
B This is Mr Pym of Technos.
A Hold the line, please. I'll see if he's there. ... Hello, Mr Pym. I'm afraid he's in a meeting. Can I take a message?
B No, thank you. Could you ask him to call me back?
A Yes, of course. Does he have your number?
B Yes, but just in case, I'll give it to you again. It's 01865 156767.
A Right, Mr Pym. I'll give him the message as soon as I see him.

Conversation Three
A Lakefield's. Good morning. Can I help you?
B Hello. Can I speak to Mr Jones, please?
A Who's calling, please?
B This is Mr Pym of Technos.
A Hold the line, please, Mr Pym. I'll see if he's there. ... . Hello, Mr Pym, I'm afraid his line's engaged. Would you like to hold?
B Yes, I'll hold.
A Mr Pym? I'm connecting you now. ...
B Hello. Is that Mr Jones?
C No, you've got the wrong extension. I'll put you through. ...
B Hello, is that Mr Jones?
D Yes, speaking.
B Ah, at last! This is Mr Pym of Technos. I'm calling you to make an appointment for next week.

6.4 Appointments

D

One
A Lawson and Fowles. Good morning.
B Good morning. This is Andrew Sands. I've got an appointment with you on Thursday at half past four.
A Yes, Mr Sands.
B Well, unfortunately I've now got an important meeting in London that afternoon. Could I change my appointment to Wednesday morning?
A Well, I'm afraid the morning's completely full up. How about Wednesday afternoon, at the same time – at four-thirty, I mean?
B Yes, that's fine. OK, Wednesday at half past four, then.

Two
A Lawson and Fowles. Good morning.
B Good morning. This is Mr Watson of EGC. I'm afraid I have a problem with my appointment next week – I'm away all week.
A Okay. Sorry did you say Mr Watson or Mr Whiteson?
B Mr Watson. W-A-T-S-O-N.
A Fine, so you're cancelling your appointment on Wednesday at 12 midday, then. Would you like to make another appointment now?
B No. I haven't got my diary here. I'll call next week.
A OK, Mr Watson. Thank you. Goodbye.

Three
A Lawson and Fowles. Good morning.
B Hello. This is Sarah Roach of Technos. I'm sorry to bother you, but it's about my appointment – the one on Thursday.
A Yes, Mrs Roach.
B Could I postpone it until later in the day? I have to collect my car from the garage.
A We've got a free slot at half past four now. Is that convenient for you?
B That's perfect. Four-thirty on Thursday. Thank you very much. Goodbye.
A Goodbye, Mrs Roach.

7

Describing and comparing

7.1 Comparing

B

A I have a meeting in Paris tomorrow evening. How long does it take to get there?
B From Central London to Central Paris it takes about three hours.
A Which is quicker, the train or the plane?
B The plane is faster. It takes about two and three-quarter hours. But you spend time checking in, boarding, clearing customs, and so on. The train through the tunnel takes about three hours twenty minutes. But you are on the train all the time, so it is easier to work for example.
A What about price?
B The train is a little cheaper. But it depends on the time of day.
A And comfort?
B Well, I am quite tall, and I think there is more leg-room on the train. It's definitely more comfortable.
A In that case, I think I'll take the train. You seem to prefer it.
B Definitely. I find it more comfortable, a bit cheaper, and usually on time.

7.2 Describing products

B

Number One

It's rectangular.
It's very thin.
It's made of plastic.
It's 8 cm long and 5cm wide.
It's multicoloured.
It's for calling from a public phone.

It's a phone-card.

Number Two

It's usually round.
It's made of metal.
It's about 70cm wide.
It's often white.
You see them on roofs of houses.
It's for receiving TV programmes.

It's a satellite dish.

Number Three

It's made of paper, and leather or plastic.
It's 20 cm long, 15 cm wide, and about 4 cm thick.
Inside there is a lot of information.
It's for keeping dates, addresses, notes, and so on.

It's a filofax.

Number Four

It's round.
It's very thin.
It's about 10 cm wide.
You put it in a machine.
It's for listening to music.

It's a compact disc.

7.3 Evaluating products

B

A Our last question today is: 'What, is the most successful product of the century?' I think the obvious answer is Coca-Cola, but I'm not sure. Jean, what do you think?
B I think one of the most successful is the Aspirin. If people have a headache, they immediately ask for an Aspirin. Aspirin cures headaches and the name is easy to remember.
C I agree, but in my opinion, the best known product of the century is the Marlboro cigarette. Probably that's because of its advertising.
A OK, so advertising is important. What about other products which exist now, but which didn't exist twenty years ago.
C There is the Walkman.
A Do you really think that is a great product?
C I think so. Millions of people buy them. They are very practical. And stylish.
B I don't agree that the Walkman is stylish. I think it is functional but not stylish. The most stylish product of the century is the Lacoste polo shirt. It is a very simple design, but it'll last for many years.
A I agree. But, again, that is because of good advertising, don't you think?
C Definitely.
A But some products are well-known without any advertising.
B Yes, like Kleenex. I'm not sure that Kleenex make all the paper handkerchiefs on the market. But it is certainly one of the most practical products of the century.
A What about children's products; games and toys, and so on?
B Lego is probably the most popular with both girls and boys, don't you think? And it seems to be popular with all ages. But there is a lot of competition so they have to continue to advertise and repackage the same idea.
A Well, I think that is a good place to end. I shall put on my Ray-Bans and go out for a Big Mac. I hope they take American Express! Until next week, goodbye.

8

Success stories

8.1 A life story

A

A Peter Parker was born in France on 30 August 1924. His father was an engineer and his mother was a teacher. He was the youngest of three sons. Both his brothers died during the Second World War.

In 1931, when he was seven years old, the family moved to Shanghai, China. They returned to England in 1937, at the start of the war between China and Japan.

In 1942, he studied Japanese on a special course for sixteen and seventeen year-olds organized by the government. He joined the army a year later. He served as an Intelligence Officer in India, Burma, and the USA, and left the army with the rank of Major in 1947.

He married Jill Rowe-Dutton in 1951. They have four children.

8.2 Lending and borrowing

D

A So, you'd like to buy a flat, Mr Regan?
B Yes, that's right.
A And how much would you like to borrow from us?
B I need a loan of £45,000.
A And what's the price of the flat?
B It's £65,000, including all the costs.
A And what about the rest of the money?
B That comes from personal savings.
A So, you have £20,000 in personal savings to invest.
B Yes, that's right.
A And when do you want to pay back the loan?
B Well, over fifteen or twenty years. It depends on the monthly repayment.
A Well, let me see. ... over fifteen years the repayment would be £420 a month, and for twenty years, it would be £390.
B I think I prefer fifteen years. What interest rate can you offer?
A At the moment, the rate is 6.6%.
B OK.
A Just one more question, Mr Regan. What's your monthly income?
B It's £625 after tax.
A £625! And does your wife work?
B No, she doesn't work at the moment – we have two young children.
B Ah. ... I think we may have a little problem here, Mr Regan.

9

Dealing with problems

9.1 Making decisions

B

A Hello, Katya. Are my travel documents ready for the trip to Bristol?
B Yes, Mrs Jarvis. You're flying to London Heathrow on a Lufthansa flight.
A What time am I leaving?
B At 13.30, arriving in London at fourteen hundred.
A And is someone meeting me at the airport?
B No, you're going on to Bristol by train. You need to take a taxi from Heathrow to London Paddington station, then the four o'clock train to Bristol.
A Is there enough time? My meeting in Bristol is at 6 o'clock.
B It's OK. The train arrives at 17.22, and the place you're visiting is close to the station.
A That's fine, then.

C

A Katya, I'm sorry. Can you change my ticket for next week? I've now got a lunch time meeting in London at 1 o'clock.
B Yes, of course. Let me get the timetable. ... OK... There's a flight from Frankfurt at 11.40, arriving at 12.15.
A No, that's too late. Isn't there a flight getting to London at about eleven?
B No, there isn't. The one before is a Lufthansa flight at half-past nine, arriving at Heathrow at ten o'clock.
A OK. I'll go on the half-past nine plane.
B Half-past nine.... OK. So, that's Flight LH 4108. And what about your train to Bristol?
A Well, I think my meeting in London will take about three hours.
B So you won't have time to catch the four o'clock train.
A No, I'll take a later train. When's the next one?
B There's one at 16.15, another at 16.45, and another at17.00.
A OK. I'll travel on the 17.00. Can you reserve me a first-class seat?
B Yes, of course.
A And I'll phone Philip Benn in Bristol to explain the problem.

9.2 Complaining

C 1

A Excuse me, but I ordered my meal half an hour ago, and I'm still waiting.
B I'm sorry about that sir.
A Could you go and see what's happening, please?
B I'll go and check in the kitchen immediately.
A Thank you. ...

B I'm sorry, sir, but it'll be another five or ten minutes. I'm afraid our usual chef is ill this evening – that's why we're a little slow.
A OK, don't worry. I'm not in a hurry.
B Shall I bring you another drink?
A Yes, please.

9.3 Thinking ahead

B

A So what do you think of the Yacht Boy 206?
B I like it. But I'm not sure about the market. Who will buy it?
A Business people, probably. They listen to the BBC on shortwave when they're away on business.
B OK. So business people working abroad will buy it. What about people *living* abroad?
A Yes, I'm sure they'll be interested. But you won't sell many to the general public, I'm afraid.
B So, as far as sales outlets are concerned, supermarkets are no good.
A No. I'm sure that supermarkets won't be interested in it. It's too specialized, and the price is too high. But I think you *will* have customers in airport gift shops.
B .... And by mail order?
A Yes, especially by mail order. That's where you'll have your best sales.
B What about advertising, then?
A Forget general magazines. You won't get good results from them. But you'll get a lot of orders if you advertise in *business* magazines. And direct mailing is the best way to attract people living abroad.
B OK, Maria. So when do I have to make a decision?
A As soon as possible!
B I was afraid you'd say that!
A No, seriously. My client wants a UK distributor as soon as possible. If you don't make a decision now, you probably won't have another chance later.
B Give me a week!
A Fine!

E

a I'll do it if I can.
b If you can't answer the question, I'll ask another person.
c I don't think I'll advertise in a business magazine.
d If we have a game of tennis, we won't arrive on time.
e I think you'll sell a lot in airports.

9.4 Apologizing

B 1

Call One

A Benn Distribution. Good afternoon.
B Hello. Can I speak to Philip Benn, please?
A Who's calling, please?
B This is Peter Van Eysen of TPS.
A Sorry. Can you spell your name?
B Yes. V-A-N new word E-Y-S-E-N.
A And I didn't catch the name of your company?
B TPS.
A Thank you. Hold the line, please... I'm connecting you.
C Philip Benn speaking.
A Hello, Mr Benn, this is Peter Van Eysen.
C Good afternoon, Mr Van Eysen. Are you calling about your order?
A Yes, about the calculators, the model RK-529. They arrived this morning, but there were no instruction manuals in the boxes.
C No instruction manuals. That's very strange.
A Can you look into the problem? And then can you call me back as soon as possible?
C Yes, of course. Do you have the order number?
A Yes, it's 4189.
C 4189. And it was twenty calculators, model RK529.
A That's right.
C OK, Mr Van Eysen. I'll call you back in 10-15 minutes.
A Can you make that 30 minutes? I'll be here at 10.
C 10 o'clock. OK. Bye.
A Goodbye.

B 2

Call Two

C Hello. Is that Mr Van Eysen?
B Yes, speaking.
C Hello, this is Philip Benn. I'm sorry about the mistake in your order. It was due to a packing error.
B Sorry?
C A mistake in packing. Somebody simply forgot to put the instruction manual in the boxes.
B So you have them at your factory. Could you send me them as soon as possible?
C Yes, of course. I'll send them today. And to compensate for the inconvenience, I'll give you a 5% discount on your next order.
B Thank you very much. And thanks for calling back.
C Not at all. Goodbye, Mr Van Eysen.

10

People at work

10.1 Suggesting and recommending

A Ugh. These sandwiches are horrible!
B They certainly are.
A I mean, look at this sandwich here. Dry bread. Three millimetres of filling. Is that real food?
B Do you know what we should do?
A What?
B We should open a sandwich shop.
A Open a sandwich shop! You're mad!
B No, I'm not. I mean a *superior* sandwich shop which sells good quality sandwiches.
A Who would eat there?
B You, me... and thousands of office workers every lunchtime.
A That's not a bad idea, you know.
B Yes. But how can we make our shop different?
A What about importing bread from France every day?
B Good idea. Everybody loves French bread. And we should only use fresh ingredients in our sandwiches – real salmon, fresh herbs, and things like that.
A People will pay a lot for something like that – we can have really high prices.
B No. I don't think we should have high prices – if we want to attract customers, our prices have to be lower than restaurants or cafés.
A Yes, you're right. So what else can we do to attract people?
B How about playing pop music in the shop? That'll attract people in.
A No, I don't think we should play pop music – it's not the right image. Classical music is better.
B Yes, I think you're right. Hey – why don't we look in the newspaper to see if there are any premises to rent near here?
A Now, just wait a minute. What about finance? Where is the money coming from?
B Let's make an appointment with my bank manager for tomorrow.

10.2 Job responsibilities

D 3

Interview One
A Do you have to travel a lot?
B Not a lot.
A Do you have to go to conferences?
B Yes, from time to time. It's important for me to know about developments in the world of science.
A And can you choose your working hours?
B Yes, I can. But it has to be between eight in the morning and eight in the evening. That's when the laboratory is open.

Interview Two
A Do you have to work in an office?
C Yes, I do, but not all the time.
A Where do you work when you're not at the office?
C I work at home. I have a computer at home, so it's no problem.
A Do you have to use the computer a lot?
C Yes, I do. When you're working with numbers and statistics, it's much quicker.
A And do you have to travel?
C Not very often. But sometimes I have to visit companies to look at their books.

Interview Three
A Can you relax at weekends?
D Not always. It's my job to find new clients, so I sometimes have to travel on Saturday or Sunday.
A Do you have to meet clients at the weekend, then?
D No, but I often fly home on Saturday. And if I'm visiting a client on Monday morning, I have to take a plane on Sunday.
A Do you have to visit clients all year round?
D No, not really. In July and August, for example, I don't have to travel much, because most companies are closed.

10.3 Correcting information

A

A Hello, and welcome to *In Business*. This week my guest is Pilar Almeida. She is 43 years old, and she works for Cygnus, a Spanish software company. She is the Managing Director of the company and, in fact, is the only woman director on the board. Pilar Almeida, welcome to *In Business*.
B Thank you very much. Er... In fact, I'm not 43 years old, I'm 47.
A Sorry about that, 47 years old. You're very honest! Now, can we just talk briefly about your early career. First, your education. You studied Business Science at the University of Madrid ...
B Yes, that's right.
A And when did you join Cygnus?
B In 1977.
A And you got your first management post two years later.
B No, not exactly. It was three years later, in 1980.
A OK. And you eventually became Managing Director in 1990?
B Yes, that's right.
A Now you are the only woman in senior management at Cygnus. Can you tell us something about the employment situation for women managers in Spain?
B Yes, of course. Well, in the public sector in Spain, 14% of directors are women, but in the private sector it is only 5%. Most women directors work in medium-sized companies like Cygnus.
A Yes, it says here that Cygnus has about 500 employees.
B No, that's not quite right. We have nearly 600, not 500. We have 500 in Spain, and 100 in the rest of Europe.
A I'm sorry – I really hope that's the last mistake today. Now, what advice can you give to women looking for ...

11

Getting a job

11.2 Applying for a job

D

1 Where do you work?
2 How long have you worked there?
3 Where do you live?
4 How long have you lived there?
5 When did you move there?
6 How long have you been here today?
7 Who is the president of your company?
8 How long has he or she been in charge?
9 Who is the Prime Minister of your country?
10 How long has he or she been in power?

11.3 The interview

B

A Thank you for coming, Mr de Oliveira. My name is Alan Green. I am in charge of Human Resources.
B How do you do?
A Do have a seat. Now then. I see you are working for Medilab at the moment. How long have you been there?
B Since 1992. It's a very interesting post, but I am looking for something with more responsibility.
A So you're ready for a change?
B Yes. I feel I have come as far as I can at Medilab and I think it is time to do something different.
A And can your family move with you easily?
B Our children are small, so it's no problem for them to change schools. My wife is a nurse, so she can find work in another part of Brazil, or even in another country.
A What kind of salary are you looking for?
B At the moment, I earn $75,000 plus a car so I would like $90,000 plus a car if possible.
A That should be fine. Have you worked abroad?
B Yes. I worked in the States for two years, and in Argentina for a year and a half. I'd like the chance to go abroad again.
A You also worked in Peru, I see.
B Yes. That was a very interesting time. We set up a vaccination programme in rural villages in Peru.

A Really? And what languages can you speak?
B Portuguese is my first language. I can also speak English, Spanish, and a little Italian.
A I'm impressed! Some of our contacts are with Japanese companies. Can you speak Japanese?
B No, I can't, I'm afraid, but I can always learn.
A Never mind! I'm now going to introduce you to our Sales and Marketing Directors for the more technical questions. I'll see you later for some aptitude and language tests.

D

A Well, Luis. I think we'll call it a day. Is there anything else you need to know?
B I don't think so. I think we have covered everything.
A I'll be in touch very soon.
B How soon?
A Oh, within a week. There are only three of you on the shortlist, so we will decide very soon. Thank you very much for coming. It was a real pleasure meeting you.
B For me as well. Thanks for everything.
A Bye bye then. Have a safe journey back.

12

Working in the nineties

12.1 Changing careers

C 2

How long did you take to find another job?
How many jobs did you apply for?
What was your first job?
When did you join Exsel Incorporated?
What did you do at Exsel?
Why did you lose your job?
How did you hear about Rochester Telephone?
What do you do at Rochester Telephone?
How long have you worked there?
Do you like your new job?

C 3

A So, Bruce, before we start the interview, I'd like to check my facts. Can I start with the details of how you looked for work? When you lost your job, how long did you take to find another job?
B Well, not too long compared with some people. Just six months.
A And I understand you applied for 600 jobs?
B No, that's not quite right. It was about 700. I remember that I sent 700 resumés.
A Seven hundred job applications in six months. That's incredible!
B Well, it's only about four a day.
A Maybe, but that's a lot of paperwork...
B Yes, I guess so.
A Well, I'd better just check the rest of my information. Can I start with your early career? What was your first job?
B Well I worked as a police officer in the 1970s.
A Really? And when did you join Exsel Incorporated?
B Just two years ago.
A So you weren't there for very long.
B No, I wasn't.
A And what did you do at Exsel?
B My complete job title was National Sales Manager. I was responsible for the domestic and the international sales force.
A And why did you lose your job?
B I lost my job because the company closed.
A Why did the company close?
B Because of heavy competition. Exsel sold computers at very low prices. When IBM and Compaq reduced *their* prices, we lost a lot of business.
A Yes, I remember the period when computer prices fell. ... Now, tell me about your new job. How did you hear about Rochester Telephone?
B From a friend. This friend knew someone in the Sales and Marketing department, and he suggested I should phone him.
A So you got the job. And what do you do in Rochester Telephone? Marketing, isn't it?
B Yes, that's right, I'm in the Marketing department. I develop new markets for phone services.
A How long have you worked there now?
B Just two months.
A And do you like your new job?
B Yes, I do. It's great to be employed again!

D

A Bruce, what advice would you give to someone who is looking for a job?
B Well, firstly – attack the problem immediately. Don't go on a long holiday – it won't help you to find a job.
A It's just wasting time.
B That's right. Secondly, work ,work ,work, on looking for a job. Before you lost your job, you did a 40-hour week, so why not now?
A So work full-time on your job applications.
B Yes, but at the same time – relax occasionally. Go to the beach, have lunch with friends, go to the gym – you need a break from time to time, even when you're unemployed.
A Useful advice. Any more?
B Yes. It's nice to meet people who are in the same situation as you – other unemployed people. You realize you are not the only unemployed person in town, and you can give each other some really good ideas.
A So you should meet people in the same position. Anything else?
B Yes. Don't apply for a job if you don't want it – be selective. If you go for an interview for a job you don't want – you're stupid! You won't get it.
A Very true. What about friends and colleagues?
B Yes, they can be very useful. Talk to them as often as possible. That's how I got my job at Rochester Telephone, from a friend.

E 1

information	situation
application	unemployment
experience	competition
manufacturing	regularly
responsible	incorporated
occasionally	immediately

E 3

the unemployment situation
manufacturing experience
he regularly makes an application
we have experience of the situation
competition is occasionally responsible for unemployment

12.3 Company culture

E

Jean-Pierre Poquet
The worst job I've ever had was when I was 21. It was my first sales job. I had to phone people at home and try and sell them encyclopaedias. If they were interested, I had to make an appointment to see them. The worst thing was that my boss was always there, listening to my phone calls. He told me I couldn't accept 'no' as an answer, and that I had to keep them talking for at least five minutes. It was terrible. Most people put the phone down after about thirty seconds. Luckily, I didn't have to visit the clients myself, my boss did that. I don't think he had any more success than me – he resigned at the same time as me!

Mercedes Villez
My worst job was in England, when I was a teacher of Spanish. It was in a school for English businessmen. I thought it was OK at first. Lessons were always in the afternoon, so I could go out and visit London in the morning. It was very strict in the school – we had to use a particular book with the students and do exactly one page per lesson – no more, no less. But that was OK too at first, because I didn't have to prepare anything. But then my students complained – not enough speaking, too much grammar, too boring! I saw the Director of the school, but he said I couldn't change my lessons or my style of teaching – that was the rule. I left a week later.

Glossary

accountant a person who keeps or checks the financial records of a business
accounts the lists of all the money that a business receives or pays
achieve to gain something; to reach an objective or goal
administration the control of a business or project
advertisement information used to sell a product or service. Abbreviations **ad; advert** – Also, to **advertise; advertising**
afford to be able to do something because you have enough money or time
agency a business that provides a particular service *(a travel agency)*
agent a person or company that represents the interests of another company in a market
annual happening or done once a year or every year *(an annual report)*
apply to ask for something in writing *(apply for a job)* – Also, an **application** *(fill in an application form)*
appointment an arrangement to see someone at a particular time
assistant a person who helps another *(an assistant manager)*
association a group of people who work together; an organization
attract to make people interested in something
automatically without being controlled by people *(The alarm switches off automatically.)*
available that you can get, buy or use *(Do you have a room available?)*
average the average of 4, 5, and 9 is 6
bank an organization that keeps money safely for its customers and lends money at interest
banknote a piece of paper money
bill a piece of paper that shows how much money you owe for goods and services
board a group of directors who control a company *(hold a board meeting)*
book to arrange to have or do something at a particular time *(I booked a single room.)* – Also, a **booking**.
borrow to take something for a short time and give it back later *(He borrowed £45,000 from the bank.)*
boss an employer; a manager
boutique a small shop that sells clothes, etc *(a fashion boutique)*
branch an office, shop, etc that is part of a larger organization *(We have branches in Paris, Milan, and New York.)*
brand the name of a product that a particular company makes *(Nescafé is a famous brand of coffee.)*
briefcase a flat case for carrying papers in
brochure a thin book with pictures of things you can buy or places where you can go on holiday *(a travel brochure)*
budget an amount of money used for a particular purpose *(an advertising budget)*
business **1** buying and selling; work *(He works in the travel business.) (Are you here on business?)* **2** a company *(a family business)*
buy-out the buying of a company by its managers, directors, etc to stop another company from taking it over *(a management buy-out)*
calculator a small electronic machine that adds, subtracts, multiplies, and divides
call to telephone someone *(I'll call you tomorrow.)* – Also, a **call**.
campaign a plan to get a special result *(launch an advertising campaign)*
cancel to decide that something you have planned will not happen *(The meeting is cancelled.)*
candidate a person who applies for a job *(I'm interviewing candidates for the marketing job.)*
capital a sum of money that you use to start a business or invest to make more money
card a piece of card or plastic that you use to pay for things *(a credit card; a phone-card)*
career a job that you train to do and do for a long time
cash to change a cheque for coins and notes *(Could I cash a traveller's cheque, please?)*
chairman **1** the head of a company **2** a person who controls a meeting
check to look at something to see that it is right *(Phone the company to check the details of the order.)*
checkout a desk where you pay a bill when you leave a hotel, a shop, etc – Also, to **check out**.
cheque a piece of paper from a bank that you sign and use to pay for things *(Can I pay by cheque?)*
client a customer; a person or company that pays for a service
colleague a person who works with you
company a business organization that sells goods or services *(I work for an insurance company.)*
compensate to pay money to someone because you have lost or damaged their property
competition the other companies who are trying to sell the same goods or services as you *(Is there much competition?)* – Also, a **competitor**. *(He says that your competitors are cheaper.)*
complain to say that you are angry about something – Also, a **complaint**
component a part of a machine *(computer components)*
computer a machine that stores information, makes calculations and controls other machines
conference a meeting, often held once a year, for people to discuss their work or interests *(I'm attending a sales conference.)*
confirm to make something definite *(Could you send me a fax to confirm your booking?)*
contact to telephone, fax, or write to someone *(Please contact me at the above address.)* – Also, a **contact** *(business contacts)*
contract a legal agreement between two people or companies *(sign a new contract)*
convenient easy or suitable *(Is Wednesday convenient for you?)*
cost to have the price of *(The tunnel cost ten billion pounds to build.)* – Also, the **cost**
customer a person who buys goods or services
CV short for curriculum vitae (Latin); information about a person's education and work experience used when applying for a new job (Am. English = **resumé**)
decide to choose something after thinking *(He decided to apply for the job.)*
delay to make someone or something late *(The flight was delayed.)*
deliver to take goods to a certain place – Also, a **delivery** *(We received delivery of the RK529 calculators this morning.)*
department a part of a company where people do a particular job *(he marketing department)*
design the way that something looks or is made; a drawing that shows this *(There are ten new designs of Swatch watch every year.)* – Also, a **designer** *(a fashion designer)*
despatch to send
destination the place where someone or something is going or being sent
develop to produce or change something *(I develop new markets for phone services.)* – Also, a **development**
director a person who controls a company or part of it *(the financial, managing, sales director)*
discount an amount of money taken off the price of something *(I'll give you a 5% discount on your next order.)*
distribute to transport and sell goods *(Philip Benn distributes electronic goods in Europe.)* – Also, a **distributor**; **distribution**

division a part of a company that deals with a certain product, service, or area *(the publishing division, the training division)*
document an official paper *(travel documents)*
due to because of *(Sales have increased due to expansion overseas.)*
earn to get money by working
economic connected with the supply of money, trade, industry, etc *(Will Europe be a top economic power?)* – Also, **economical** = costing less money, time fuel *(an economical car to run)*; **economy** = saving money *(travel economy class)*
EC Abbreviation for European Community
EEC Abbreviation for European Economic Community
effective producing the result you want *(an effective form of advertising)*
electronic of computers and silicon chips *(transfer information by electronic means)* – Also, **electronics**; **electronically**
employ to pay someone to do work for you *(The company employs 50,000 people worldwide.)* – Also, **employment**; employee = a person who is paid to work; employer = a person or company that pays other people to do work
enclosed put in an envelope with a letter *(The contract is enclosed.)* Abbreviation **enc**.
engaged (of a telephone) in use *(I'm afraid his line's engaged.)*
engagement an arrangement; an appointment
engineer a person who designs, builds or repairs machines – Also, **engineering**
estimate to calculate the cost, size, etc of something approximately
evaluation deciding how good someone or something is *(All staff have regular performance evaluations.)* – Also, to **evaluate**
exchange to give or receive something in return for something else
executive a person who makes important decisions in a company
expand to become bigger (We are expanding into Eastern Europe.) – Also, **expansion**
exports goods sent abroad. – Also, to **export**
facilities buildings, equipment, etc that make it possible to do something (Ecospar has childcare facilities.)
factory a building where goods are made *(a car factory)*
fact something that is true *(company facts and figures)*
fax a letter or message sent by a fax machine using telephone lines. *(Send me a fax to confirm the booking.)* – Also, to **fax**
filofax a small book for keeping dates, addresses, etc in
financial connected with money *(the financial director)*
first-class the best quality *(travel first-class)*
fixed-term for a limited time only *(a fixed-term contract)*
franchise a business that has permission to make or sell named goods
full-time for the whole of a normal period of work *(a full-time job)*
functional practical and useful rather than attractive *(a functional design)*
goods things for sale *(electronic goods)*
group a number of companies *(the ICL Group)*
headquarters the main office of an organization (Abbreviation = **HQ**)
high-quality of a good standard; well made *(high-quality products)*
import to buy goods from abroad
income money that is earned from work, sales or investments
incorporated of a registered company. Abbreviation **Inc**.
industry **1** making things in factories **2** all the companies that make the same thing *(the motor industry)* – Also, **industrial**
ingredient one of the items used to make things to eat *(We use only fresh ingredients in our sandwiches.)*
inspection the act of looking at something closely to check that it is done correctly *(All our suppliers have regular inspections.)*
institute an organization, especially one involved in teaching or research
insurance an agreement in which, in return for a regular payment, a company agrees to pay a sum of money to someone who is injured or whose property is lost or damaged *(medical insurance)*
interest money charged for borrowing money
interview a meeting is which someone is asked questions *(a job interview)* – Also, to **interview**; an **interviewer**
invention a thing that is made for the first time *(The computer is a great twentieth-century invention.)*
invest to spend money in order to make a profit, for example by buying machinery for a factory, or shares in a company
invoice a list of goods sold with prices that is a demand for payment
itinerary a plan for a journey or visit, showing places, dates, times and people to see
job work that you do to earn money
journalism writing news for newspapers, radio or television – Also, a **journalist**
launch to introduce a new product or company to the market
licence an official document that allows you to do something *(a driving licence)*
line a telephone connection *(I'm afraid his line's engaged.)*
list names, items, etc written or printed *(Where can I find a list of hotels.)*
loan a sum of money borrowed from a bank
loss the money lost by a business
maintenance keeping machines, etc in working order
manage to control and organize a business or part of it – Also, a **manager**; **management**
manpower the people you need to do a particular job
manual **1** using your hands *(manual workers)* **2** a book that tells you how something works *(an instruction manual)*
manufacture to make something in large quantities using machines *(We manufacture computers.)* – Also, **manufacturing**; **manufacturer** *(a watch manufacturer)*
market a geographical area, or section of the population, where you can sell products *(We operate in six different target markets.)*
marketing deciding how something can be sold most easily, eg what price it should be or how it should be advertised
market share the percentage of the total sales of a product in a particular area obtained by one company
MBA short for Master of Business Administration
mechanism a piece of equipment or machine that does a certain task *(The watch has a quartz mechanism.)*
meeting an occasion when people come together to discuss something – Also, to **meet**
memo a note sent from one person to another within an company. Formal = **memorandum**
memory the part of a computer where information is stored
message written or spoken information that is passed from one person to another
model a particular type of machine, car, etc made by a certain company
mobile phone a telephone without wires that you can carry with you
notepad sheets of paper in a block that are used for writing notes
offer to give or provide something. *(We offer a 5% discount.)* – Also, an **offer** *(a job offer)*
office a room or building where work is done
officer a person with a position of authority or responsibility in an organization *(a personnel officer; a police officer)*
operate **1** to do business *(ICL operates in six different target markets.)* **2** to work a machine – Also, an **operator** *(a switchboard operator)*
opportunity a chance to do something or have something that you want *(an opportunity for promotion)*
option a choice, an alternative
order a request for goods – Also, to **order**
organize to plan or arrange something – Also, **organization**; **organizer**
outlet a place where goods can be sold *(sales outlets)*
owe to be in debt
own to possess; to have as your property
pack to put things in boxes, containers, etc ready for sale
package a parcel
paperwork the written work that you do in an office
part-time for part of the normal working week *(a part-time job)*
pay to give money in return for goods and

services – Also, **payment**
PC Abbreviation for personal computer
per each *(Her budget is £150 per night.)*
percentage a part of an amount, expressed in hundredths of that amount *(What percentage of people work at home?)*
personal of or belonging to a particular person *(personal savings)*
personnel **1** employees, staff. **2** the part of a company that deals with recruitment and training
pharmaceutical connected with the production of medicines *(a pharmaceutical company)*
photocopy to make copies of letters, etc using a photocopier – Also, a **photocopy**
portable that you can carry easily *(a portable video)*
portfolio a list of investments that a particular investor has
position a job
postpone to delay; to put something off until a later time or date
potential possible *(potential clients)*
predict to say what you think will happen – Also, a **prediction**
presentation the act of showing or talking about something
private sector the parts of a country's economy that are owned by a person or company, not by the state
product something that you make to sell – Also, **production**; to **produce**
profit the money made by a business – Also, **profitable** = making a profit
professional connected with your work or career
promote **1** to give someone a more important job. **2** to advertise a product – Also, **promotion**; **promotional**
public relations the work of distributing information to give a good impression of an organization
publicity advertising
public sector the part of a country's economy that is owned by the state
publishing the business of producing books, computer software, etc for sale
purchase to buy
qualified having the right education and experience for a job *(a qualified accountant)* – Also, a **qualification**
quality how good or bad something is *(high-quality products)*
quantity a number or amount
range a group of products sold by one company
rate the level of something *(interest rates)* or how fast something happens *(a growth rate)*
Re *(in a letter)* short for 'with reference to'
receipt a document that shows you have paid for something
reception a meeting place in a hotel or company – Also, a **receptionist** a person who receives visitors to a hotel or company
recession a fall in economic activity
recommend to suggest, to speak well of someone or something
recruit to employ or take on new staff
recycling treating used material so that it can be used again *(a paper recycling company)*
redundant without work, not needed – Also, **redundancies** = job losses
reduce to make something less or lower (reduce prices) – Also, a **reduction**
reference a statement or letter that describes a person's character
regulations rules
rent to hire, to borrow something in return for money – Also, **rent** the money paid to rent something
reorganization to organize something again so that it is more efficient *(Following our reorganization, the group now consists of 29 autonomous companies.)*
repackage to change the way a product is presented for sale
repay to pay back money that you have borrowed – Also, **repayment**
report a written or spoken statement about an event, meeting, etc – Also, a **reporter** a person who writes for the newspapers or gives out news on radio or television
representative a person who speaks for a organization, especially to promote and sell their products. Abbreviation **rep** – Also, to **represent**
research a careful and detailed study of something – Also, to **research**
reservation a booking. *(a hotel reservation)* – Also, to **reserve**
resign to give up or leave a job
resource something that a person or country can use, for example oil
restructuring changing the way a company, etc is organized
resumé see CV
retail the selling of goods to the public
retire to stop working at the end of a career, usually between the ages of 55 and 65 – Also, **retirement**
risk something that might cause a loss or danger
salary a monthly payment for doing a job
sales the amount sold
samples small quantities of a product that show what the rest is like
schedule to arrange for something to happen at a particular time *(a scheduled flight)*
scheme a plan or system for doing or organizing something
secretary a person who types letters, makes appointments, answers the phone, etc in an office
sector a part of the economy of the country *(the private sector, the public sector)*
security **1** something of value that can be claimed by a bank, etc if a loan is not repaid *(He offered his life insurance as security.)* **2** things you do to protect people and places from attack *(a security guard, a security pass)*
service a job or system that provides things people need *(room service, a taxi service, financial services)*
set up to begin or establish something *(We set up a vaccination programme in Peru.)*
share **1** a fraction or part of something *(We have increased our market share by 5%.)* **2** a part of a company. *(The parent company owns 82% of the shares.)* – Also, a **shareholder** a person who owns shares.
short-list a list of choices, for example candidates for a job, selected from a longer list
sign to write your name on a document, cheque, etc
skill a thing that you can do well, that you need for a job, etc *(computer skills, management skills)*
slogan a short phrase that is easy to remember *(advertising slogans)*
software programs that you use to operate a computer
solution an answer to a problem
specialize to concentrate of one type of product or activity *(We specialize in high-quality coffees.)*
spend to pay money for something. *(How much do you spend on advertising?)*
staff all the people who work for a company
standard a level of quality
state-of-the-art the newest, the most modern. *(This computer is the state-of-the-art.)*
statistics numbers which have been collected in order to provide information about something
status your social or professional position *(marital status)*
stock goods in storage waiting to be sold – Also, to **stock**.
store a large shop
strategy a plan that you use in order to achieve something
strike a time when people refuse to work, usually because they want more money or better working conditions
structure the way something is organized or built *(company structure)*
stylish fashionable and attractive *(a stylish design)*
subsidiary a company that is owned by another company
successful having achieved what you wanted *(a successful product, a successful company)*
supervisor a person who directs and checks the work of others
supply to provide customers with goods or services – Also, a **supplier**
survey a study of something – Also, a **surveyor** a person who examines a building or land to find out how much it its worth *(property surveyors)*
switchboard the place in an organization where all the telephone calls are connected *(a switchboard operator)*
system a group of things or parts that work together *(a railway control system)*
target a result that you want, a place or thing that you aim at *(We operate in six target markets.)*
tax money that a person or company pays to the government
technical relating to machines *(a technical problem)*
technology the study and use of science for

industry – Also, **technological**

teleworking (Am. telecommuting) working at home and communicating with other people using computers – Also, a **teleworker**

temporary lasting a short time; not permanent *(a temporary job)*

timetable a list of times when things happen *(a train timetable)*

total counting everything *(Total sales were $1.2 billion.)*

train to teach – Also, **training** *(staff training)*

transfer to move from one place to another

transport buses, cars, planes, etc that carry people and things *(They travelled by public transport.)*

trial a test *(drug trials)*

trip a journey (a business trip)

turnover the total sales of a company *(Our turnover for this year is $250 million.)*

unauthorized without official permission *(No admittance to unauthorized personnel.)*

unemployed not having a job – Also, **unemployment**

The authors and publisher would like to thank the following for their permission to reproduce photographs and illustrative material:

3M United Kingdom PLC: p. 97 (Scotch TapeTM, and Post-It®)
Agnès B. UK Ltd.: p. 20 (Agnès B) / Thierry Lefèbure
Apple Computers (UK) Ltd/Firefly Communications: p. 97 (Power Mac)
Aurora & Quanta Productions, Lovell: p. 146 (Bruce Kulp by Peter Essick)
Barreto Photography, New York: p. 102 (Kenshin Oshima)
BASF PLC: p. 11 (logo)
Bausch & Lomb U.K. Limited: p. 97 (Ray-Ban sunglasses)
British Broadcasting Corporation: p. 11 (logo), p. 20 (Alan Yentob)
Boeing UK: p. 97 (Jet)
The British Petroleum Company PLC: p. 11 (logo)
Canon (UK) Ltd: p. 92 (desk copier)
Columbia Sportswear: p. 105 (G Boyle and T Boyle), p. 106 (jacket)
Eurotunnel: p. 90 (shuttle)
Guinness Brewing Worldwide Ltd: p. 95 (logo)
Grundig International Ltd.: p.115 (radio)
ICL plc: p. 11 (logo), p. 50 (building)
JVC (UK) Limited: p.11 (logo)
Levi Strauss & Co/Shilland & Co Ltd: p. 97 (jeans)
McDonald's Restaurants Ltd.: p.95 (logo) / Warren Potter
Marks & Spencer PLC: p.62 (Linda Dawson), p. 67 (shops)
Mars Confectionery: p. 95 (logo)
Polaroid (UK) Limited: p. 97 (camera)
Pret a Manger: p. 122 (restaurant)
The Radisson Empire Hotel: p. 28 (lobby)
The Randolph Hotel: p. 38 (hotel interior)
Rover Cars: p. 97 (Mini Cooper)
The RTZ Corporation PLC: p. 11 (logo)
SmithKline Beecham: p. 97 (Tabasco® Pepper Sauce). Made in the USA by McIlhenny Co. Avery Island, Louisiana, Tabasco® is a registered trademark.
Sony United Kingdom Limited: p. 97 (Walkman)
J. Stainton/WPA: p.152 (Julian Stainton)
Starbucks Coffee Company: p. 13 (logo and store)
Swatch SA: p. 16 (watches, Nicholas Hayek) / A.D. Euqster
Vaka Helgafell HF, Iceland: pp 8-9 (Olaf Olafsson)
Volvo Car UK Limited: p. 95 (logo)
Waddingtons Games Ltd.: p. 97 (Monopoly, © 1994 Tonka Corporation. All Rights Reserved). Manufactured and distributed in the United Kingdom under licence by Waddingtons Games Ltd. Leeds, Monopoly® is a registered trademark.

The publishers would also like to thank the following for their permission to reproduce photographs:

Ace Photo Library/Ian Allenden, Chris Arthur, John Baker, Senka Causevic, Clare Coe, Arthur Mauritius, Mugshots, Gabe Palmer, Pete Rushton, Alexis Sofianopoulos
Andes Press Agency/Carlos Reyes-Manzo, Fujifotos
Art Directors/Jed Share
Hulton Deutsch Collection/Steve Eason
Image Bank/Campolungo, David De Lossy, J Freis, Robert J Herko, Steve Niedorf, Schmid-Langsfeld
Oxford Picture Library/Chris Andrews
Rex Features
Sally and Richard Greenhill
Science Photo Library/James King-Holmes, Philippe Plailly, Jerrican Sittler
Tony Stone Images/Doug Armand, Simon Battensby, Dan Bosler, Paul Cenward, Cosmo Condina, Joe Cornish, Nicholas De Vore, Laurence Dutton, Wayne Eastep, Shaun Egan, Elizabeth Furth, Michael Harris, Frank Herholdt, Tif Hunter, Mitch Kezar, Ian Murphy, Dennis O'Clair, Jon Ortner, Joseph Pobereskin, Donovan Reese, Loren Santow, Charles Thatcher

Cover photographs by:
Tony Stone Images/Simon Battensby, Dennis O'Clair, Charles Thatcher

Illustrations by:

Kathy Baxendale 11; Ken Binder 50, 108; Brett Breckon 43, 44; Nicki Elson 55; John Gilkes; Peter Gudynas 144, 149; Pantelis Palios 30, 40, 101, 125, 132; Andy Nightingale; Mike Ritchie 152, 153; Colin Salmon 27, 45; Tim Slade 49; Alex Tiani 111; Sholto Walker/Garden Studio 56, 73, 151

Studio and location photography by:

Rob Judges, John Walmsley

Design by:

Shireen Nathoo Design

Art editor:

Kate Wheeler

Acknowledgements

The authors and publisher would like to thank the following for permission to use adapted material and/or reproduce copyright material in this book:

Agnès B. UK Ltd. (p. 20)
Columbia Sportswear, Baltimore (pp. 105-6)
The Telegraph plc for graphic 'How Times Compare with Rivals' © The Telegraph plc, London, 1994, from the Daily Telegraph, 6 May 1994 (p. 89)
Linda Dawson of Marks and Spencer, London (p. 62)
The European Ltd for bar charts from 'Lifestyle Survey', The European, Oct 1992 (p. 22)
Eurotunnel, the Channel Tunnel Concessionnaires (p. 90)
Fortune for two graphics from Fortune magazine, 4 April 1994
Fujitsu Ltd. Tokyo
Grundig International Ltd. (p. 115)
ICL plc (pp. 50, 58-9)
KPMG Peat Marwick, New York, for adapted extracts from New York Hotels Directory (p. 26)
Bruce Kulp of Rochester Telephone Corporation (p. 146)
Marks & Spencer PLC (pp, 62, 67)
Olafur J. Olafsson of Sony Electronic Publishing Company, New York (pp. 8-9)
Kenshin Oshima of Shohkoh Fund & Co., Ltd. Tokyo (p. 102)
Pantheon Books, a division of Random House, Inc. for front cover illustration of *Absolution* by Olafur Johann Olafsson.Translation copyright © 1994 by Olafur Johann Olafsson.
Sir Peter Parker (pp. 98-9)
Pret a Manger, Julian Metcalfe and Sinclair Beecham (p. 122)
The Radisson Empire Hotel, New York (p. 28)
The Randolph Hotel, Oxford (p. 38)
Society of London Theatre for adapted map of London theatreland (p. 45)
Julian Stainton of Western Provident Association Ltd. (pp. 152-3)
Starbucks Coffee Company, Seattle (p. 13)
Swatch SA, Zürich & Biel (p.16)
Alan Yentob of BBC Televison (p. 20)

Although every effort has been made to trace and contact copyright holders before publication, this has not always been possible. If notified, the publisher will be pleased to rectify any errors or omissions at the earliest opportunity.

The authors would like to thank the following people:

The staff and shareholders of ILC Group;
The teachers and students at ILC Paris and ILS Nantes;
Company clients Roussel Uclaf, Rhône-Poulenc, Total, GAN, and others who have helped us define and redefine the material our students need;
Jon Goodliffe and Andrew Hutchinson for their collaboration right at the start;
Libbie Herbert and Sue Gaston for the restaurant game;
Penny McLarty and Heidi Grant for advice and encouragement;
Our editors for showing us how to turn our ideas into a book.

The authors and publisher are very grateful to everyone who commented on the course during its preparation, particularly the following:

David Biermann, Hohenfels
Deirdre Brero, Lyon Langues, Lyon;
Robyn Christensen, Schering AG, Berlin;
Patricia Crook, Formation et Communication, Paris;
Josephine Ezzarouali and Karen Carnet, LOGOS, Grenoble;
Eamonn Fitzgerald, Munich
Simon Gardner, Lanser S.A., Bilbao;
Guy Heath, LinguaSec, Madrid;
Kevin Lewis, EADA, Barcelona;
Clare O'Dolan, Unilangues, Paris La Défense;
Jan Pulford, Market Place, Grenoble;
Brendan Conor Quain, Secretariado Internacional, Oviedo;
Alan Ross, Englisch Studio, Nürnberg;
Sally Senior, Inlingua, Frankfurt;
Jeremy Townend, InfoLangues, Lyon;
Rennie Tracy, Unilangues, Paris La Défense.

The authors

David Grant is the Principal of International Language Services, Nantes.
Robert McLarty is the Managing Director of International Language Centres (France).

Oxford University Press
Walton Street, Oxford OX2 6DP

Oxford New York
Athens Auckland Bangkok Bombay
Calcutta Cape Town Dar es Salaam Delhi
Florence Hong Kong Istanbul Karachi
Kuala Lumpur Madras Madrid Melbourne
Mexico City Nairobi Paris Singapore
Taipei Tokyo Toronto

and associated companies in
Berlin Ibadan

ISBN 0 19 457208 0

First published 1995

Printed in Hong Kong